# THE JERKY BIBLE

# THE JERKY BIBLE

## How to Dry, Cure, and Preserve Beef, Venison, Fish, and Fowl

# KATE FIDUCCIA

Skyhorse Publishing

Skyhorse Publishing books may be purchased in bulk at special discounts for sales promotion, corporate gifts, fund-raising, or educational purposes. Special editions can also be created to specifications. For details, contact the Special Sales Department, Skyhorse Publishing, 307 West 36th Street, 11th Floor, New York, NY 10018 or info@skyhorsepublishing.com.

Skyhorse® and Skyhorse Publishing® are registered trademarks of Skyhorse Publishing, Inc.®, a Delaware corporation.

Visit our website at www.skyhorsepublishing.com.

10

Library of Congress Cataloging-in-Publication Data is available on file.

Cover design by Laura Shaw
Cover photo credit: Thinkstock

Print ISBN: 978-1-62914-554-9
Ebook ISBN: 978-1-63220-010-5

Printed in China

Dedication

To the loves of my life—Peter and Cody.

# Other Books by Kate Fiduccia:

- *Venison Cookbook*
- *Cabin Cooking*
- *Grillin' and Chili'n'*
- *Backyard Grilling*
- *Cooking Wild in Kate's Kitchen*
- *Cooking Wild in Kate's Camp*
- *The Quotable Wine Lover*

# Contents

# An Introduction to Jerky

## What is Jerky?

There are many meanings of the word jerky. Some are funny, such as when someone acts jerky. Some relate to articles of clothing. A jerkin is a short, tight-fitting piece of clothing worn by women. But we're concerned with the food-related terminology for jerky. Jerky is meat or fish that has been sliced or formed in thin strips and prepared carefully for preservation. About one pound of raw meat yields four ounces of jerky. Jerky even includes fruit and vegetables.

Before we delve into jerky and jerky making, there is a difference between drying and preserving meat and making meat jerky. When drying meat that will be rehydrated later on, the meat has to be cooked first then dried. When meat has been cooked and dried, it can be stored in the freezer for up to one year. Meat jerky, which does not always require that it is cooked, can be stored in zip-top bags for two to six months.

## Why Jerky Today?

Many people are returning to the basics and are enjoying the art of preparing their own food. Many are also concerned about being able to control what goes into their food products and the food preparation process. Other food lovers are making jerky from their own beef, game meat, or poultry to save money. Jerky has also seen a resurgence in popularity as a quick nutritional snack for athletes, dancers, and long-haul truckers alike. It's also an integral part of the Paleo diet, whose followers try to emulate the eating patterns of our caveman ancestors.

## History of Jerky

Jerkied meat and fish have been a part of every culture's history. Some say it had its origins with the ancient Incas. The Incas had an advanced method of food preservation and storage. Because they were able to store and hold food much longer than any other people at that time, they were able feed their armies and extend their influence along the route of the Camino de Las Incas to reach the Pacific Ocean on the west and through the Amazon jungles on the east. The Incas usually used llama or alpaca meat that was freeze-dried and stored. They called this dried meat "charqui" (charkey), which then came to be known in English as "jerky."

Ancient Egyptian civilizations also had jerky as a food source. In addition to drying strips of meat from game animals indigenous to Northern Africa, they dried fish as well.

Our first Native Americans made jerky out of buffalo meat. They used their buffalo jerky as a staple to tide the tribe over through the long winter months and also valued it for its ability to be carried as they traveled from one place to another. When the first settlers came to the New World, they were introduced to jerky, as well as a variation of jerky called pemmican. Pemmican is traditionally prepared from venison (buffalo, moose, elk, or deer). The meat is cut into thin slices and dried out in the sun or over a low fire until nearly all the moisture is gone. The ratio of raw meat to final pemmican product is five to one. Once the meat is dried, it is pounded into a fine substance almost like powder. Then it is mixed with melted fat at a ratio of about one to one. Oftentimes, dried fruits, such as blueberries or cranberries, that have also been pounded into a powder-like substance are mixed in, as well. The final mixture was then formed into portion-sized pieces or stored in rawhide pouches.

Native Americans who lived near the ocean would soak the strips of meat in salt water before drying. This is one of the earliest forms of brining food. An alternate method of making jerky was over fire. Used to either keep the flies off the meat or keep the meat dry with a fire inside a large teepee, the smoke from the fire added flavor to the jerky.

As the early settlers headed west, traders and explorers valued this food source, as fresh food was often scarce during their travels. They also realized it as a viable food option once game was killed and the fresh meat ran out. The meat of other game animals was also made into jerky, such as turkey, goose, duck, and even fish.

With today's varied options for preparing jerky, nearly any low-fat food product can be made into jerky. Traditional jerky meats include beef, buffalo, deer, caribou, moose, antelope, rabbit, and lamb. Poultry jerky includes chicken, turkey, duck, ostrich, and emu. Freshwater fish jerky includes bass, walleye, sunfish, and crappies. Saltwater fish jerky includes sole, flounder, rock cod, trout, catfish, and salmon. The end goal for all these types of jerky is to produce a safe shelf-stable product that has had nearly all of its moisture removed so it can be stored without refrigeration.

## Jerky Safety
### *When is it Safe to Eat?*

Jerky safety is a pertinent concern since raw meat or fish is the primary ingredient. Special care must be taken to drastically reduce the moisture content to inhibit any bacterial growth. In 1995, for example, nearly a dozen people in Oregon became ill after eating *E. coli* tainted homemade jerky.

*E. coli* is a type of bacteria that normally lives in the intestines of people and animals. There are, however, a few types of *E. coli*, particularly *E. coli* 0157:H7, that can cause intestinal infection. The more common infection symptoms include diarrhea, abdominal pain, and fever. In cases that are more severe—usually in people with weakened immune systems—one can have bloody diarrhea or even kidney failure.

Most whole meat jerky is prepared and dried at temperatures of 140 to 155°F. At these temperatures, most of the moisture is extruded, but the temperature is not hot enough to kill the bacteria if there are any. When making ground meat jerky, there is a greater chance of bacterial contamination. Since the meat went through a grinder, any pathogens that were present on the machinery have been distributed through the mixing process. Furthermore, any bacteria that may have been only on the surface of the meat are mixed into the product.

Other pathogens to be concerned about include *Salmonella* and *Trichinella*. The *Trichinella* parasite was found in cougar jerky that was prepared and consumed in 1995. Remember that for anyone to become sick from eating jerky, there are three things that have to happen. Bacteria or pathogens have to be on the meat. The meat is then prepared in a manner that does not kill the bacteria. Lastly, the meat is consumed with the bacterial contamination.

Jerky is safe to eat when all the pathogens are eliminated and the product is shelf stable. Shelf stable is when a product can be stored at room temperature without supporting any microbial growth.

There are three methods that can be used to prepare jerky so it is free of pathogens. While they are effective, they are not typically used when making jerky, as the end product often has a different feel and taste than your typical jerky. Three of the most effective ways to prepare jerky and ensure that the pathogens have been eliminated include:

*Vinegar Soak*: Raw meat that is to be made into jerky is soaked in vinegar. Then these strips are marinated in a seasoned sauce or dry rub. Lastly, the meat is dried in an oven, dehydrator, or smoker. The combination of the vinegar's acid properties and the dry heat result in the elimination of pathogens.

*Post-Drying Heating*: Dried meat strips are placed in a low-heat oven (about 275°F) for about ten minutes to kill the bacteria.

*Precooking the Meat*: Raw meat slices are dipped in a hot brine. The slices may be removed once they reach an internal temperature of 160°F. This method also reduces the pathogens on the meat.

### When is it Dry?

Sufficient moisture in a food product serves as a basis for microorganisms to grow. Research has determined that shelf-stable beef jerky has a moisture content of 0.85 or less. To prevent mold growth on jerky, it should have a final moisture content of 0.70 or lower. Tools to measure the moisture content of jerky products are not available to consumers, but there are other measures to use to check for doneness.

Most times, when the meat is well-dried, it is dark and fibrous and will be brittle enough to break when bent in half.

## Factors that Affect Cooking/Drying Time

Factors that affect the drying time vary widely depending on the type of product you are using, its shape, thickness, fat content, and the amount of air circulation in your dehydrator or oven, as well as the consistency of the unit's temperature.

To ensure a cooking time that will apply to all the pieces of meat, have them as similar in size and in thickness as possible. On average, most jerky strips are cut to about 1 inch wide, about ⅜ to ¼ inch thick, and about 6 to 10 inches long. The more uniform they are, the better chance that they will all be done at the same time.

Whole meat strips of jerky that have been in a liquid marinade will take longer to dry than those that have had a dry seasoning applied. The same holds true for the ground meat jerky that has had just a dry seasoning versus a liquid one mixed in. Generally, a ground meat jerky that has been formed with a jerky gun will take a shorter time to dry than whole meat jerky.

The more consistent the temperature and air movement in your oven or dehydrator, the better and quicker the drying time. Jerky needs moisture to be removed, and the circulating air removes the moisture that rises to the surface as the meat dries. A consistent temperature in the oven will ensure a better product overall. Too low of a temperature will not cook or dry the meat sufficiently, and too high of a temperature will cook the outside and make it brittle.

Lastly, ambient air conditions also affect the drying and storing times. Making jerky in an oven in the humid areas of the Southeastern United States will take a bit longer than doing this in the arid regions of the Southwest.

## Lean Versus Fatty

Since fatty cuts of meat will turn rancid, always select the leanest cuts of meat. If you are going to buy beef at the store, USDA select grade is leaner and will have less internal fat, or marbling, than choice or prime grade cuts. If you use ground beef for jerky, use as lean a mixture as possible, preferably 93 percent lean or higher. Grass-fed beef, as a whole, is much leaner than corn-fed or grain-fed beef. So, ideally, this type of beef will have a lower fat content to begin with. All venison is leaner than beef. The best cuts to use include the loin, round, and flank.

Some wild game, including wild hogs, cougar, and bear meat, can be infected with the parasite known as *Trichinella*. Freezing and drying these meats will not kill this parasite. But the pre cooking method—when the meat reaches an internal temperature of 160°F—will kill these parasites and most other pathogens.

### Poultry and Rabbit

The leanest cuts of poultry and rabbit are the breast of poultry and the loin of rabbit. Trim all cuts of skin and fat before marinating or drying.

### Fish

Lean fish are the best for making jerky. Some of the leaner fish, with less than 2.5 percent fat, include:

- Cod
- Flounder
- Grouper
- Haddock
- Mahi-Mahi
- Monkfish

- Perch
- Pollock
- Red Snapper
- Sea Bass
- Sole

It is common, however, to see recipes for salmon jerky, and there are two in this book. The key to safely making jerky out of fattier fish is to include some time in a smoker so the heat from the woody smoke assists to remove as much fat from the fish as possible. This is not necessary all the time.

Fish needs less time to marinate. The flavors of a marinade or rub will penetrate the flesh in less time than with other meats.

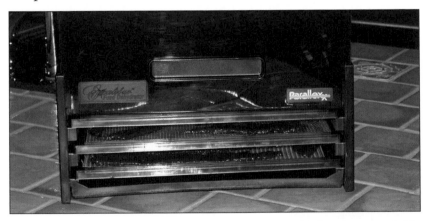

This dehydrator is made of hard plastic and comes with four trays, a dial to control the thermostat, and a fan. Be sure that the front door closes completely when drying jerky.

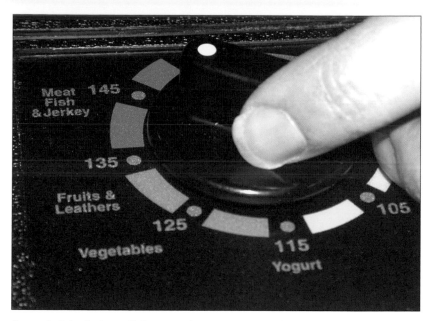

A good dehydrator will have a thermostat control with settings for various types of foods.

## How to Dry Jerky

*Dehydrator*

Electric dehydrators are the most commonly used method to make jerky. They vary in capacity (wattage), fan speed, and air movement—some are vertical and others are horizontal. There is a wide variance in the efficiency of home dehydrators. Some take longer than others to reach the desired temperature. Others have temperatures that fluctuate during the drying process. Some are not calibrated to match what is set on the temperature dial. In the end, look for the best dehydrator that you can afford and one that has the following features:

- A dial to control the thermostat with temperatures between 130 and 150°F. The proper temperature for producing safe jerky is between 145 and 155°F. It is not advised to use a dehydrator with preset temperatures that you cannot control.
- A fan to distribute air throughout the entire unit.

- Food-grade or stainless steel trays.
- Outside construction made of steel, hard plastic, or aluminum, along with double-wall construction to minimize any heat loss.
- Enclosed heating element.
- Instruction manual.
- Sufficient number of trays.

### *Conventional Oven*

A conventional oven is a good tool for making jerky. Many folks use this method—but it usually takes a bit longer than a dehydrator since there is no air movement within a traditional oven. With the process taking longer, the oven-drying method for making jerky also uses more energy.

You should be sure that your oven is calibrated correctly to its thermostat. You want to make sure that if you set it for about 145 to 155°F that the oven stays at that temperature for quite awhile. To test for this, set the oven at 150°F and place an oven thermometer inside on a rack in the middle of the oven. Be sure to prop the oven door open as if you were making jerky. Check the thermometer at half-hour increments to make sure it stays at the desired temperature. If your oven doesn't maintain a consistent temperature, do not use it for making jerky. If the oven is too hot, the jerky product may get too crisp on the outside and the interior moisture will not evaporate. If the oven is inconsistently cold, then it may not get hot enough to properly dry the jerky product, which may spoil. Lastly, remember to put a pan or foil on the bottom of the oven to catch any potential drips from the meat.

By propping the door open on your oven, you will be able to increase the air movement inside. This will help to dry out the product.

### Camp Jerky

Jerky can also be made the old fashioned way—but with a few provisos! For those who love to turn back the clock and try tasks the way they had to be done before modern times, making jerky out in the sun or near a campfire can be fun. Mind you, it will take much longer and will require much more attention than making it in your kitchen oven or dehydrator. So, if time is on your side, give it a try.

To make jerky in a conventional oven, set the oven at its lowest temperature. If it does not have a setting at about 150°F, set it at its lowest temperature, put an oven thermometer inside, keep the door slightly open, and check to see how low the oven temperature gets.

There are a few precautions you must pay attention to when making camp jerky. First, the humidity must be low. Remember that even when you are making jerky in a controlled situation—with a kitchen oven, smoker, or dehydrator—the goal is to minimize the moisture content of the meat. When the air conditions outside are humid, this goal will be a tough one to achieve. So keep an eye out in the forecast for some dry days when the humidity is at its lowest in your area. If you live in a naturally arid area, you have this first concern taken care of. Second, you will need to hang the jerky strips in an area without flies or other insects that can contaminate the meat. If you have a spot where there is a good breeze, this will help. Keep in mind that as air circulates around the pieces of meat, it removes moisture from the outside surfaces. Third, if you choose to make jerky over or near a fire, you will need to balance the heat and smoke from the fire. You want to have sufficient heat to dry out the meat strips but not cook them. You will also want a fair amount of smoke from the fire to add some flavor to the meat. If your jerky is not done by sun down, be sure to cover the jerky or put it in a covered area overnight. You do not want moisture of any kind to contact the jerky before it is done. Fourth, to minimize bacterial contamination and growth, be sure you have plenty of salt on your meat or have marinated it well in a salty brine.

This is a box-style electric smoker, which is an ideal size if you are just starting out. It has double walls and a stainless steel interior.

To keep your cleanup to a minimum, cover the top of the wood box with foil. Line the bottom of the smoker with foil, as well.

Smokers have a variety of uses and can be set to higher temperatures for larger cuts of meat and fish. Make sure the smoker you choose has a lower setting for making jerky.

As you can see from previous photos of my older Cookshack model, smokers can be a part of your outdoor kitchen for a long time. Above is an image of their newest version of the Smokette Original—same quality product, just an updated version!

### Smoker

Because the temperature of a smoker is between 140 and 200°F when making jerky, it is often called cool smoking. A box-style electric smoker is an ideal unit for making jerky this way. A box-style smoker typically has well-insulated walls, and this feature helps keep the cooking temperature consistent throughout the process. If you are using a smoker with uninsulated aluminum walls, be wary that the temperature could fluctuate greatly depending upon the weather temperature and conditions outside.

One of the easiest things to do when you get a new smoker is make jerky. Making jerky in a smoker is simple and rather quick. The key to making jerky this way is to keep in mind that the smoke will be adding flavor to the meat. Be careful not to over smoke or add too much smoke flavor to the meat. A shortcut to making jerky with a smoker is to let the meat cook in the smoker for several hours, then finish the process in a dehydrator.

When using an electric smoker, you'll need to use fine wood. The heating plates in electric smokers usually don't get hot enough to ignite large pieces of wood. Smoking sawdust is an ideal form of wood to use with an electric smoker. Several manufacturers sell smoking sawdust, including www.thesausagemaker.com, www.lemproducts.com, www.butcher-packer.com, www.askthemeatman.com, and www.meatprocessingproducts.com.

### Microwave

Making jerky in a microwave is not easy to do if you want to achieve similar results as to when making it in an oven, dehydrator, or smoker. The principle behind a microwave is that the waves sent through the oven move the water particles of a food item back and forth. As the water particles rotate rapidly, they produce energy. This energy, in turn, raises the temperature of the food and cooks it. That's why one of the best features of a microwave is reheating already cooked foods.

When we make jerky, we are trying to dry out the meat while raising its temperature slightly. We do not want to cook the meat per se. So, trying to achieve this balance in a microwave can be difficult. The few times I have tried making jerky in a microwave, the results were not something I fed to my human counterparts! You may have better success with a convection microwave, where the air in the microwave gets moved around to help dry out the product.

## Meat for Jerky

The main goal in making jerky is to produce a shelf stable product with as little moisture as possible, because of this it is easiest to work with lean cuts of meat and fish. Furthermore, since meat has both lean and fatty parts, it's crucial to keep the fatty parts to a minimum, as these will turn rancid over time. For the best end product with the longest shelf life, choose the leanest cuts of beef, venison, poultry, lamb, and fish.

The top sirloin cut of beef is an ideal cut for making whole meat jerky. This is typically a leaner cut of beef than other cuts. Here you can see the grain of the meat. For chewy jerky, cut the slices with the grain. For more brittle jerky, cut the slices against the grain. (Photo courtesy New York Custom Processing, LLC www.newyorkcustomprocessing.com)

### Whole Meat Jerky

Most jerky is made from whole cuts of meat. From about four pounds of fresh whole meat, you will yield one pound of great tasting jerky. To make slicing easier, use a piece of meat that is slightly frozen. Slice the meat into long thin strips that are about ⅜ to ¼ inch thick, about 1 inch wide, and 6 to 10 inches long. This, of course, will vary depending upon the size of the whole meat you are cutting. Whether you are using a large or small piece of whole meat, keep the cuts or strips as uniform in size as possible. This will help keep the cooking time the same for all strips.

When starting with whole meat jerky, trim the meat of all fat and connective tissue. Continue to do so as needed as you cut the meat into strips. If you like jerky that is a bit chewy, cut the slices with the grain of the meat. If you like jerky that is more brittle yet tender, slice it against the grain.

### Ground Meat Jerky

Just as it sounds, ground meat jerky is made with ground meat that has been flavored and also has either salt or a preservative in it. Typically, ground meat jerky is quicker to make than whole meat jerky, it's tastier, and oftentimes is easier to chew. There are a variety of ground meat jerkies to make, including ground beef, venison, turkey, and chicken.

As with whole meat jerky, use ground meat that is 90 percent lean or leaner. If you will be making your own ground meat for jerky, be sure to remove all the fat and connective tissue from the meat before grinding.

Jerky guns help to simplify making jerky out of ground meat. It doesn't take too much practice to get the hang of making strips that are the same length. The various tips of the gun can output either flat strips or round sticks. With either tip, there is no concern of making strips or sticks with consistent thickness.

You must pay attention to food safety when making your own ground. The grinding machine, bowls, cutting utensils, and your hands must be sanitized to minimize any bacterial contamination. Use a mixture of half a teaspoon of concentrated bleach (8.25 percent sodium hypochlorite) or a teaspoon of regular bleach (6 percent sodium hypochlorite) per quart of warm water when washing.

The salt added to the ground meat not only helps to draw out moisture, but it also helps bind the ground meat together. I have used a jerky gun with ground meat jerky. The jerky gun ensures even thickness and width of the strips. It's up to you to determine how long the strips are. You can also press ground meat between two pieces of wax paper and flatten it with a rolling pin. Once flattened to the thickness of your liking, you can make strips out of the pressed ground meat.

## Making Jerky

### Marinades, Brines, and Cures

Jerky making includes pretreating the meat or fish. The primary purpose of a marinade when making jerky is to add flavor. Marinades also help to tenderize food. When a marinade contains acidic foods, such as lemon juice, tomato juice, vinegar, or pineapple juice, these ingredients help break down the tissues of tough meat. If you are using a tender cut of meat, such as a cut from loin or sirloin, and you want to add flavor, be careful not to use a marinade with a lot of acid. Too much acid or marinating a tender piece of meat too long may break down the protein fibers too much, and the meat becomes mushy. When marinating meat, use a glass or plastic dish rather than one made out of aluminum or metal. Many acidic ingredients react with metals and will give the food an off flavor. A zip-top plastic bag also works well for marinating meats. Place the meat and the marinade in the zip-top bag. Squeeze out the air and roll the bag with the meat and marinade at the bottom of the bag. Close the zip-top bag when it is rolled up to get as much air out of the bag as possible. Turn the bag from time to time to make sure the marinade is getting to all the surfaces of the meat.

A brine is a salty, sugary mixture that is meant to add moisture to a piece of meat or poultry. But when making jerky, brines are often used to add salt to a piece of meat or fish. In *Jerky* by A.D. Livingston, he includes a recipe for Brine-Cured Smoked Jerky with Rub. This recipe begins with immersing meat in a brine made with salt, molasses, and other spices for eight hours or so. Then, he puts a dry rub on the strips and smokes the jerky. This is a delicious combination of methods and flavors for making jerky.

A standard brine consists of one part salt to eight parts water. This ratio varies depending upon the size of the meat or fish being brined. If you are brining a large cut of meat, the ratio of salt to water should be higher. From this basic recipe for brine, you can add other herbs or flavorings to your taste. Some like to simply brine a piece of meat and then make jerky. Others like to use the brining as a first step before continuing on with either marinating or adding a rub to add flavor.

When marinating meat, use either a glass or plastic bowl. A bowl or dish made out of aluminum or metal may react to the marinade and impart an off flavor to the meat.

Always place your marinated meat, fish, fowl, or other food products in the refrigerator for the required length of time to let the flavors set in. Keeping the food product cold will keep bacterial growth to a minimum.

### Salt

Salt helps reduce bacterial growth in meat. When our ancestors first dried meat and fish, they often used seawater or the salt from seawater. There are different types of salt and salt products available today to aid the jerky-making process. Morton Tender Quick is a good curing salt blend. This blend consists of plain salt, sugar, curing agents, and other compounds to maintain a uniform mixture. When keeping food safety and minimizing bacterial growth uppermost in mind, I like to use Morton Tender Quick as often as possible. Other salts include canning or pickling salt, kosher salt, and table salt. Canning or pickling salt and kosher salt do not have added curing agents, so the chance of bacterial growth is greater. Table salt contains iodine, and some say that this can give a slight off flavor to a brine.

### Adding Flavor

Adding flavor to your jerky can be as simple as seasoning the strips with garlic salt and pepper. Press the seasonings into the meat strips and let them sit in a cool environment. Or you can also add flavor with a paste or dry rub. A simple paste could consist of freshly crushed garlic, dried oregano, and thyme with a few drops of olive oil.

### Commercial Products

One of the simplest and rather fail-proof ways to begin making jerky is to use a commercially made marinade or rub. There are plenty available on the market, and they come in a wide variety of flavors and seasonings. If you are a novice jerky maker, using a commercially available seasoning is an excellent way to create a base flavor and texture for your final product from which you can judge all your own creations. Most of the jerky-making products include excellent instructions, safe food-handling techniques, and ingredients (such as nitrite for ground meat jerky).

There are many commercial products available for making jerky. If you are just beginning, try some of the ready-made seasonings for marinating. Once you know your seasoning preferences, you can make your own marinades.

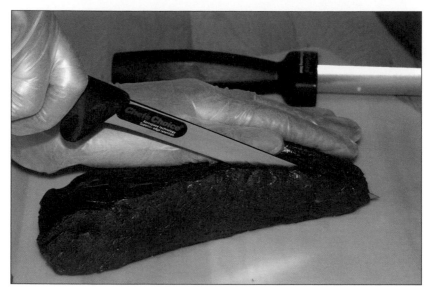

When working with any raw food products, it's a good idea to wear food safety gloves. This is especially important when mixing ground meats.

### Safe Food Handling When Making Jerky

When I was an undergrad at Cornell University's Hotel School in the 1980s, one of the required courses was Food Sanitation (which later became Food Microbiology). For some reason, which still eludes me today, I was drawn to the topics covered in this class, such as the whys of food-borne illnesses, learning about bacteria and other pathogens naturally found in food, etc. I even went on to be one of the teaching assistants in later semesters. Since those fond years (oh so many years ago), I have always kept food safety in mind, whether I was developing recipes for my cooking segment on our television show Woods N, Water, writing wild game and fish cookbooks, giving wild game cooking demos at sports shows, running a restaurant, and even now as I manage a USDA custom beef processing plant in upstate New York. My habit of using food service gloves and keeping a spray bottle with bleach water in the kitchen has passed on to friends, family, and even our son, Cody. He, too, now keeps the same kind of spray bottle in his kitchen to minimize contamination.

So, when you make jerky, you're handling raw food. Either use food service gloves or wash your hands with soap and warm water when handling raw food. As you wash your hands, sing a full verse of "Happy Birthday." Once the song is done, you have washed long enough and can rinse and wipe your hands dry.

If you will be handling different kinds of meat, either use different cutting boards or clean one cutting board well before using it again. I like the thin, pliable plastic cutting boards. I have six or eight of them in my kitchen. I place one on top of my large wood cutting board, use it, fold it slightly to dispense the meat into a bowl or plastic bag, then drop the plastic board into my sink. I usually keep a few inches of hot soapy bleach water in the sink for the initial soak of the plastic cutting boards. If you use only one cutting board, wipe it clean, spray it with a bleach mixture, and then wash and dry it thoroughly before using it again.

A proper bleach solution is one tablespoon of chlorine bleach to one quart of water.

# RECIPES

As with any cookbook you read, the recipes can be followed to a T, or if you like to give something your own flair, you can use the recipes as a guideline. And so it is with jerky recipes. You'll soon learn if you like to make jerky with meat sliced with the grain (chewy) or against the grain (more brittle). You'll make a more experienced call when it comes to the length of time that you let a piece of meat or fish marinate, as well as how long you need to have the product dry before it is done to your liking.

With that said, following are some jerky recipes for all types of meat, fish, fowl, fruits, and some to make your own pet jerky treats. Enjoy!

# BEEF JERKY
# Chili Beef Jerky

This recipe combines the use of a smoker and a dehydrator. The smoker adds a wonderful flavor to the jerky, then the dehydrator completes the drying process.

Prep Time: 15 minutes
Marinating Time: 8 to 24 hours
Drying/Smoke Time: 4 to 5 hours
Yield: About ¼ pound jerky

### Ingredients
- 1 pound top round steak or sirloin lean steak, trimmed and cut into long thin strips about ¼ inch thick
- ⅓ cup Worcestershire sauce
- ½ cup low sodium soy sauce
- ¼ cup brown sugar
- 4 cloves garlic, crushed
- 2 teaspoons fresh ground black pepper
- 2 teaspoons ground dried red chili
- 1 teaspoon cumin
- 1 teaspoon onion powder

### Preparation
1. Combine all ingredients except the meat in a non metallic bowl and mix well. Add meat strips and mix well. Pour the marinade and the meat into a zip-top bag, remove as much air as possible, and marinate for 8 hours or overnight in the refrigerator.
2. Prepare smoker for a 4-hour smoke at about 150°F. Mesquite or oak wood works well with this recipe. After meat has marinated, pour meat into a strainer, allowing all of the marinade to drain from the meat. Discard marinade. **DO NOT REUSE!** Blot the meat strips dry on paper towels.

3. Lay out the meat strips on a sheet of foil. Spread out the meat evenly. Place in smoker and smoke until the surface begins to blacken or about 3 hours. Cover the strips loosely with foil. The purpose of the foil is to minimize the smoke but to let as much moisture evaporate as possible. Continue smoking for 1 to 2 hours. Meat should be well dried. At this point, test the strips. If they still have quite a bit of moisture and need to dry more, you can continue to dry the beef jerky in a food dehydrator or an oven on a very low temperature.

4. When the jerky is done, it will crack but not break when bent.

---

### SMOKING WOODS

Depending upon the type of jerky you plan to make, here is a listing of some of the more popular woods and their flavors that can be used when making jerky:

**Apple** – Mild, sweet, slightly fruity, strongest flavor of all the fruitwoods. Can be mixed with oak and cherry for a nice blend of flavors. Works well with poultry and game birds.

**Ash** – Light yet distinctive flavor. Works well with venison.

**Cherry** – Like apple, a bit sweet, fruity smoke, but with deeper tones and heavier flavor. Can be mixed with apple and oak woods. Works well with venison and beef.

**Chestnut** – A tad sweet and nutty flavor. Good with venison and beef.

**Hickory** – A favorite smoking wood. A heavy, strong bacon flavor that works with beef and venison. To cut down on the bitter taste, soak the wood a few hours before smoking. Or mix it with oak to cut down the hickory flavor.

**Maple** – A bit sweet, yet mildly smoky flavor. Great with poultry and game birds.

**Mesquite** – Another favorite smoking wood. Sweet with a pinch of bitter flavor. Works well with beef, fish, and poultry.

**Oak** – Similar to mesquite but lighter in flavor with little or no aftertaste. Good with almost anything you want to smoke, including beef, venison, and fish.

**Peach** – Milder and sweeter than hickory yet sweet and woodsy. Great with turkey, chicken, and game birds.

**Sugar Maple** – Smoky and mellow. Goes well with meat and fish.

**Other Flavored Smoke Woods** – Retailers have a variety of woods that either have had flavors added to them or were previously soaked in them. Some retailers sell wood from old whiskey barrels, old wine barrels, etc. Try them and see what flavors they add to your foods.

# Asian BBQ Jerky

Prep Time: 20 to 30 minutes
Marinating Time: 6 to 24 hours
Drying Time: 4 to 6 hours
Yield: ¼ to ½ pound jerky

## Ingredients

- 1 to 2 pounds lean beef, top round or eye round
- whole pink, white, and black peppercorns, cracked
- ½ cup soy sauce
- 1 tablespoon sesame oil
- 1 tablespoon sesame seeds, black and tan
- 2 tablespoons brown sugar
- ½ of a grated pear or apple
- ½ onion, sliced thinly
- 2 to 3 cloves garlic, minced
- 1 teaspoon grated fresh ginger

## Preparation

1. Trim the meat of all fat and connective tissue. Slice the meat into ¼- to ⅜-inch thick slices. Rub the cracked peppercorns into the meat strips.

2. In a large non metallic bowl, combine the remaining ingredients. Mix well. Add in the meat pieces and stir to cover the slices with the marinade. Cover the bowl. Place in refrigerator for 6 hours or overnight. Stir from time to time to ensure that all slices are covered by the marinade.

3. After meat has marinated, pour meat into a strainer, allowing all of the marinade to drain from the meat. Discard marinade. **DO NOT REUSE!** Blot the meat strips dry on paper towels. Place meat on dehydrator trays or oven racks making sure not to allow the strips of meat to touch. Allow the strips to dry in the oven (150 to 170°F) or electric dehydrator (145 to 150°F). When the jerky is done, it will crack but not break when bent.

# Four Star Beef Jerky

This beef jerky recipe has a savory blend of flavors that knocks this one out of the park!

Prep Time: 10 to 15 minutes
Marinating Time: 8 to 24 hours
Drying Time: 4 to 6 hours
Yield: About ½ pound jerky

## Ingredients

- 2½ pounds lean beef, top round sirloin, trimmed of all fat and connective tissue, cut along the grain into strips about ¼ inch thick and 4 inches long. It will be easier to slice if it is slightly frozen
- ⅛ cup fish sauce
- ¼ cup sugar
- ¼ cup oyster sauce
- 1 tablespoon coarsely ground black pepper
- 1 tablespoon garlic powder
- 5 cloves garlic, slightly crushed
- ½ tablespoon salt

## Preparation

1. Place all ingredients except the meat and sesame seeds in a sturdy zip-top plastic bag. Close bag. Hold bag securely at the top, shake vigorously to mix ingredients well. Open bag, add meat, and shake vigorously until meat is well covered. Allow to marinate in refrigerator for 8 to 12 hours, turning bag frequently.
2. Drain meat well. Discard marinade. **DO NOT REUSE!** Blot the meat strips dry on paper towels.
3. Place meat on dehydrator trays or oven racks, sprinkle with sesame seeds making sure not to allow the strips of meat to touch. If drying in an oven, preheat the oven to 250°F.
4. Allow the strips to dry in the oven (150 to 170°F) or electric dehydrator (145 to 150°F). When the jerky is done, it will crack but not break when bent.

# Peppered Cola Jerky

Prep Time: 30 to 40 minutes
Marinating Time: 6 to 12 hours
Drying Time: 4 to 6 hours
Yield: About ½ pound of jerky strips

### Ingredients

- 2 pounds beef top round, partially frozen
- ¾ cup Coca-Cola
- ⅓ cup low sodium soy sauce
- 1½ tablespoons Worcestershire sauce
- ⅓ cup plain rice vinegar
- ¼ cup maple syrup
- 5 tablespoons ground black pepper
- 1 chipotle chile, chopped
- ⅓ cup onion, diced
- ⅔ teaspoon ground red pepper
- 4 whole black peppercorns
- 2 tablespoons fresh garlic cloves, minced

### Preparation

1. In a saucepan, whisk together Coca-Cola, soy sauce, Worcestershire sauce, rice vinegar, maple syrup, and 2 tablespoons fine black pepper. Wisk sauce and bring to a full boil. Reduce sauce to a simmer for 10–15 minutes or until slightly reduced. Remove from heat, let cool.
2. Add chilies, diced onions, fine red pepper, black peppercorns, and minced garlic to sauce. Wisk sauce to combine, cover with plastic, and let sit.
3. While the sauce sits, trim excess fat and any connective tissue from the sirloin steak. Cut jerky strips along the grain of the meat about ¼ to ⅜ inch thick.
4. Place meat strips into a large zip-top plastic bag, add sauce, remove air from bag, and seal. Marinate beef strips 6 to 8 hours or overnight. Turn bag over a few times to marinate beef strips evenly.
5. Drain meat well. Discard marinade. **DO NOT REUSE!** Blot the meat strips dry on paper towels.

6. Place meat on dehydrator trays or oven racks, making sure not to allow the strips of meat to touch. About half way through the cooking time, sprinkle the strips with the remaining ground pepper.
7. Allow the strips to dry in the oven (150 to 170°F) or electric dehydrator (145 to 150°F). When the jerky is done, it will crack but not break when bent.

It is easier to slice whole meats when they are partially frozen. Try to maintain even thickness of the slices so they all dry at the same time.

# Sechuan Beef Jerky

Prep Time: 20 to 30 minutes
Marinating Time: 8 to 24 hours
Drying Time: 4 to 6 hours
Yield: ¼ pound jerky

**Ingredients**

- 1 pound lean beef, loin or sirloin
- ½ cup smooth peanut butter
- ¼ cup canola oil
- ¼ cup hot chili oil
- 1 teaspoon chili powder
- 2 tablespoons lime juice
- ½ teaspoon five spice powder
- 2 tablespoons fresh ginger, minced

**Preparation**

1. Combine all ingredients except the beef in a small bowl. Mix well with a spoon.
2. Trim excess fat and any connective tissue from the cut of beef. Cut jerky strips along the grain of the meat about ¼ to ⅜ inch thick.
3. Place sirloin strips into a large zip-top plastic bag, add sauce, remove air from bag, and seal. Massage marinade into the beef strips to cover them thoroughly. Marinate beef strips 6 to 8 hours or overnight. Turn bag over a few times to marinate beef strips evenly.
4. Drain meat well. Discard marinade. **DO NOT REUSE!** Blot the meat strips dry on paper towels.
5. Place meat on dehydrator trays or oven racks making sure not to allow the strips of meat to touch.
6. Allow the strips to dry in the oven (150 to 170°F) or electric dehydrator (145 to 150°F). When the jerky is done, it will crack but not break when bent.

# Bordeaux Beef Jerky

Prep Time: 20 to 30 minutes
Marinating Time: 8 to 24 hours
Drying Time: 4 to 6 hours
Yield: ¼ pound jerky

**Ingredients**

- 1 pound lean cut of beef, loin, sirloin, or rump, all fat and connective tissue removed
- ½ cup Bordeaux red wine
- ¼ cup balsamic vinegar
- ½ cup olive oil
- 1 tablespoon Dijon mustard
- 2 tablespoons Herbes De Provence (this is a savory blend of rosemary, thyme, oregano, basil, marjoram, and fennel seed)
- 2 cloves garlic, minced
- 1 teaspoon cardamom
- 1 teaspoon sea salt
- 1 teaspoon freshly ground black pepper

**Preparation**

1. Combine all ingredients except the beef and a portion of the ground pepper in a small bowl. Mix well with a spoon.
2. Trim excess fat and any connective tissue from the cut of beef. Cut jerky strips along the grain of the meat about ¼ to ⅜ inch thick.
3. Place sirloin strips into a large zip-top plastic bag, add sauce, remove air from bag, and seal. Massage marinade into the beef strips to cover them thoroughly. Marinate beef strips 6 to 8 hours or overnight. Turn bag over a few times to marinate beef strips evenly.
4. Drain meat well. Discard marinade. **DO NOT REUSE!** Blot the meat strips dry on paper towels.
5. Place meat on dehydrator trays or oven racks making sure not to allow the strips of meat to touch. About halfway through the cooking time, sprinkle the strips with the remaining ground pepper.
6. Allow the strips to dry in the oven (150 to 170°F) or electric dehydrator (145 to 150°F). When the jerky is done, it will crack but not break when bent.

# Maple Sage Beef Jerky

Prep Time: 20 to 30 minutes
Marinating Time: 8 to 24 hours
Drying Time: 4 to 6 hours
Yield: ½ pound jerky

## Ingredients

- 2 pounds lean beef, loin, sirloin, or rump, all fat and connective tissue removed
- ¼ cup balsamic vinegar
- 2 tablespoons low sodium soy sauce
- ¼ cup pure maple syrup
- 1 tablespoon Morton's Tender Quick salt
- 1 teaspoon dried sage
- 1 tablespoon orange zest
- ½ teaspoon garlic powder
- ¼ teaspoon freshly ground black pepper

## Preparation

1. Combine all ingredients except the beef in a small bowl. Mix well with a spoon.
2. Trim excess fat and any connective tissue from the cut of beef. Cut jerky strips along the grain of the meat about ¼ to ⅜ inch thick.
3. Place sirloin strips into a large zip-top plastic bag, add sauce, remove air from bag, and seal. Massage marinade into the beef strips to cover them thoroughly. Marinate beef strips 6 to 8 hours or overnight. Turn bag over a few times to marinate beef strips evenly.
4. Drain meat well. Discard marinade. **DO NOT REUSE!** Blot the meat strips dry on paper towels.
5. Place meat on dehydrator trays or oven racks making sure not to allow the strips of meat to touch. About halfway through the cooking time, sprinkle the strips with the ground pepper.
6. Allow the strips to dry in the oven (150 to 170°F) or electric dehydrator (145 to 150°F). When the jerky is done, it will crack but not break when bent.

# Easy Beef Biltong

Biltong is a South African version of American beef jerky. It has been a staple of the country for more than four hundred years. Traditional biltong is made from wild game, including wildebeest, kudu, ostrich, and the like. It can be made into thick strips or flat thin pieces. It also is traditionally dried out in the open with only the sunlight as the source of heat. In the recipe below, a dehydrator is used to better control the drying of the meat.

Prep Time: 10 to 20 minutes
Marinating Time: 1 hour
Drying Time: 4 to 6 hours
Yield: ¼ to ⅓ pound biltong

## Ingredients
- 1 pound lean beef, top sirloin, or loin
- 2 tablespoons rock salt
- ½ cup apple cider vinegar
- ½ teaspoon ground cardamom
- 1 tablespoon coarse ground black pepper
- 1 tablespoon ground coriander

## Preparation
1. Trim excess fat and any connective tissue from the cut of beef. Cut jerky strips along the grain of the meat about ¼ to ⅜ inch thick.
2. Sprinkle rock salt on both sides of the strips of meat. Place in the refrigerator for one hour.
3. Remove the meat from the refrigerator and scrape off all the excess salt with a knife.
4. Place the vinegar in a small bowl. Dip each of the meat slices into the vinegar briefly and set aside. Sprinkle cardamom, ground pepper, and ground coriander over the meat on all sides.
5. Place meat on dehydrator trays or oven racks making sure not to allow the strips of meat to touch.
6. Allow the strips to dry in an electric dehydrator (145 to 155°F). When the biltong is done, it will crack but not break when bent.

# David's Hamburger Sausage Jerky

David Gould shared this recipe with me. He is an avid upstate New York hunter and he has been creating, tasting, and sharing wild game dishes for many years. While the end product resembles that of small sausage rolls, the technique is similar to making jerky. Enjoy!

Prep Time: 5 to 10 minutes
Marinating Time: 4 days
Drying Time: 10 hours
Yield: 3 sausage jerky rolls

## Ingredients

- 5 pounds lean ground hamburger
- 5 tablespoons Morton's Tender Quick salt
- 2½ teaspoons mustard seed
- 2 teaspoons peppercorn and coarse ground pepper
- 2½ teaspoons garlic salt
- 1 teaspoon hickory smoked salt or mesquite liquid smoke
- 1 tablespoon of crushed red pepper flakes if you prefer a spicy taste

## Preparation

1. Mix all ingredients thoroughly. Refrigerate.
2. Knead the mixture once per day for three days.
3. On the fourth day, knead very well. Make three rolls about 2½ inches wide by about 6 inches long. Place them on a baking sheet, preferably lined with non stick aluminum foil.
4. Bake at 150°F for 10 hours. Let cool. The sticks can be frozen after cooling.

# VENISON JERKY

The term venison is broadly defined as the meat from any game animal, including but not limited to the deer and its relatives, but also bear, antelope, wild boar, peccary, and more. For the purposes of this cookbook, however, venison refers to the more customary group of deer, elk, caribou, and moose meat.

One of the prime benefits of venison is its low fat content. With only 3.6 grams of fat in a four-ounce piece of meat*, venison is one of the healthiest meats available today. In addition, wild venison has not been injected with preservatives, hormones, antibiotics, or other substances associated with certain health risks.

Feel free to interchange various venison meats. You can substitute deer venison with caribou venison and so on. Be careful with wild boar (*Brucella suis*), cougar, and bear meats, as they can carry *Trichinella* worms. They are slightly higher in fat content and can carry organisms that can be harmful to humans. To be on the safe side, I generally do not make jerky out of these types of wild game.

Several of the jerky recipes in this book have been contributed by an avid wild game cook, Helen DeFreese. Helen's roots are from the South and while she has honed her wild game and fish cooking expertise in New York, many of her southern traditions and styles shine through in her recipes. Helen was a dedicated part of our Woods N' Water team with Peter and me for more than ten years when we lived downstate. We were fortunate enough to taste her many creative dishes and jerky treats through the years.

---

*Source: US Department of Agriculture

# Italian Ground Venison Jerky

Prep Time: 5 to 10 minutes
Marinating Time: 4 days
Drying Time: 10 hours
Yield: About 2 dozen jerky sticks

## Ingrediants
- 3 pounds of ground venison, no added fat
- 3 tablespoons of Morton's Tender Quick salt
- 1 teaspoon freshly ground pepper
- 2 teaspoons garlic powder
- 1 teaspoon dried oregano
- 1 teaspoon dried basil
- 1 teaspoon dried marjoram

## Preparation
1. Mix all ingredients in a large bowl and knead well. Let sit in the refrigerator covered with plastic wrap for 1 to 2 days.
2. Remove the meat mixture from refrigerator, knead well. Line a large rimmed baking sheet with nonstick foil or parchment paper. Place meat mixture on the large rimmed baking sheet. With a rolling pin, roll out the ground meat mixture to fill the sheet pan so the meat is about ¼ inch thick.
3. Lightly score the flattened mixture for the size of the jerky sticks you want.
4. Place in a pre heated oven set at 150°F and let bake for about 8 to 12 hours. About halfway through, flip the meat mixture over onto a sheet pan of the same size also lined with nonstick foil or parchment paper. Place the mixture back in the oven. Check after another 2 hours for doneness.
5. When the jerky is done, it will crack but not break when bent. Extra jerky strips can be frozen.

# Honey Lola Sweet Venison Jerky

Prep Time: 30 minutes
Marinating Time: 24 to 48 hours
Drying Time for Oven: 4 to 6 hours
Drying Time for Electric Dehydrator: 5 hours
Yield: 1 pound dry jerky

## Ingredients

- 4 pounds venison meat, roast, tenderloin, or any cut of meat is fine
- 6 teaspoons salt
- 2½ teaspoons black pepper
- ½ teaspoon garlic
- 1 cup brown sugar
- 1¼ cups soy sauce
- ¾ cup Worcestershire sauce
- 1 cup BBQ sauce
- ½ cup honey

## Preparation

1. Rinse meat thoroughly in cold water to remove any remaining hair, blood, or other foreign matter. Trim all fat, tallow, and silver skin completely from meat. Cut the meat with the grain approximately into ¼- to ½-inch thick strips depending on your preference.
2. Combine all the ingredients above except meat in a non metallic container. I suggest a plastic bowl with an airtight lid. Mix well.
3. Place sliced meat in container with marinade and mix well making sure all of the meat is thoroughly covered. Refrigerate container for 12 to 24 hours, stirring often.
4. After meat has marinated, pour meat into a strainer, allowing all of the marinade to drain from the meat. Discard marinade. **DO NOT REUSE!** Blot the meat strips dry on paper towels. Place meat on dehydrator trays or oven racks making sure not to allow the strips of meat to touch.
5. Allow the strips to dry in the oven (150°F with oven door slightly ajar) or electric dehydrator (145°F). When the jerky is done, it will crack but not break when bent.

# Hot to Trot Venison Jerky

Helen's husband Brian is an avid angler and hunter. There is no end to the variety of game meats and fish that he brings home for Helen to prepare for the entire family. This is one of his favorite jerky recipes.

Prep Time: 30 minutes
Marinating Time: 12 to 24 hours
Drying Time for Oven: 4 to 6 hours
Drying Time for Electric Dehydrator: 5 hours
Yield: 1 pound jerky

**Ingredients**

- 4 pounds of venison
- 6 teaspoons salt
- 3 teaspoons black pepper
- ½ teaspoon garlic
- ½ cup brown sugar
- 1¼ cups soy sauce
- ½ cup BBQ sauce
- ½ cup plus 2 tablespoons Worcestershire sauce
- 1 to 2 teaspoons crushed red pepper flakes
- ½ teaspoon cayenne pepper

**Preparation**

1. Rinse meat thoroughly in cold water to remove any remaining hair, blood, or other foreign matter. Trim all fat, tallow, and silver skin completely from meat. Cut the meat with the grain approximately into ¼- to ½-inch thick strips depending on your preference.
2. Combine all the ingredients except the meat in a non metallic container. I suggest a plastic bowl with an airtight lid. Mix well.
3. Place sliced meat in container with marinade and mix well making sure all of the meat is thoroughly covered. Refrigerate container for 12 to 24 hours, stirring often.
4. After meat has marinated, pour meat into a strainer, allowing all of the marinade to drain from the meat. Discard marinade. **DO NOT REUSE!** Blot the meat strips dry on paper towels. Place meat on dehydrator trays or oven racks making sure not to allow the strips of meat to touch.
5. Allow the meat strips to dry in the oven (150°F with oven door slightly ajar) or electric dehydrator (145°F). When the jerky is done, it will crack but not break when bent.

# South of the Border Jerky

Because this recipe is on the hot side, make a small batch to begin with. If it meets your liking, just double up the meat and other ingredient portions. But be careful with the jalapeño and Tabasco portions—you may want to just increase them slightly.

Prep Time: 20 minutes
Marinating Time: 12 hours
Drying Time for Oven: 4 to 6 hours
Drying Time for Electric Dehydrator: 5 hours
Yield: ¼ pound jerky

## Ingredients
- 1 pound lean deer meat, such as sirloin or rump
- 1 teaspoon Jalapeño juice
- 1 teaspoon Tabasco sauce
- 3 teaspoons salt
- 1 teaspoon black pepper
- 2 tablespoons soy sauce
- ½ cup French dressing

## Preparation
1. Rinse meat thoroughly in cold water to remove any remaining hair, blood, or other foreign matter. Trim all fat, tallow, and silver skin completely from meat. Cut the meat with the grain approximately into ¼- to ½-inch thick strips depending on your preference.
2. Combine all the ingredients except the meat in a non metallic container. Mix well.
3. Place sliced meat in container with marinade and mix well making sure all of the meat is thoroughly covered. With this smaller batch of jerky, you could also use a plastic zip-top bag. Mix the meat and the marinade well. Roll the bag up to push all extra air out of the top. Seal the bag closed. Refrigerate the mixture for 12 hours, stirring or turning the bag often.
4. After the meat has marinated, pour the meat into a strainer, allowing all of the marinade to drain from the meat. Discard

marinade. **<u>DO NOT REUSE!</u>** Blot the meat strips dry on paper towels. Place meat on dehydrator trays or oven racks making sure not to allow the strips of meat to touch.

5. Allow the meat strips to dry in the oven (150°F with oven door slightly ajar) or electric dehydrator (145°F). When the jerky is done, it will crack but not break when bent.

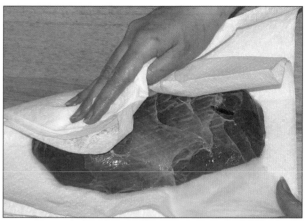

# Fast and Easy Teriyaki Jerky

Prep Time: 15 minutes
Marinating Time: 8 to 12 hours
Drying Time for Oven: 4 to 6 hours
Drying Time for Electric Dehydrator: 5 hours
Yield: 1 to 1½ pounds of dry jerky

## Ingredients

- 5 pounds venison meat, preferably a sirloin or round cut
- 6 ounces Teriyaki sauce
- 4 ounces soy sauce
- 2 teaspoons black pepper

## Preparation

1. Rinse meat thoroughly in cold water to remove any remaining hair, blood, or other foreign matter. Trim all fat, tallow, and silver skin completely from the meat. Slice meat into ¼ -to ½-inch thick strips across the grain.
2. Place all ingredients except the meat in a sturdy zip-top plastic bag. Close bag. Hold bag securely at the top, shake vigorously to mix ingredients well. Open bag, add meat, and shake vigorously, until meat is well covered. Allow to marinate in refrigerator for 8 to 12 hours, turning bag frequently.
3. Drain meat well in a strainer. Discard marinade. **DO NOT REUSE!** Blot the meat strips dry on paper towels.
4. Place meat on dehydrator trays or oven racks making sure not to allow the strips of meat to touch.
5. Allow the strips to dry in the oven (150 to 200°F with oven door slightly ajar) or in an electric dehydrator (145°F). When the jerky is done, it will crack but not break when bent.

# Onion and Garlic Lover's Jerky

Prep Time: 20 to 30 minutes
Marinating Time: 8 to 12 hours
Drying Time for Oven: 4 to 6 hours
Drying Time for Electric Dehydrator: 5 hours
Yield: 1 to 1½ pounds of dry jerky

## Ingredients

- 4 to 6 pounds lean venison, loin, sirloin, or rump meat
- 2 tablespoons salt
- 2 teaspoons onion powder
- 1 onion, minced
- 1 shallot, minced
- 3 teaspoons garlic powder
- 2 teaspoons black pepper
- 1 cup Worcestershire sauce
- ½ cup soy sauce
- 2 teaspoon crushed red pepper flakes

## Preparation

1. Rinse meat thoroughly in cold water to remove any remaining hair, blood, or other foreign matter. Trim all fat, tallow, and silver skin completely from the meat. Slice meat into ¼- to ½-inch thick strips with the grain.
2. Place all ingredients except the meat in a sturdy zip-top plastic bag. Close bag. Hold bag securely at the top, shake vigorously to mix ingredients well. Open bag, add meat, and shake vigorously until meat is well covered. Allow to marinate in refrigerator for 8 to 12 hours, turning bag frequently.
3. Drain meat well in a strainer. Discard marinade. **DO NOT REUSE!** Blot the meat strips dry on paper towels.
4. Place meat on dehydrator trays or oven racks making sure not to allow the strips of meat to touch.
5. Allow the strips to dry in the oven (150 to 200°F with oven door slightly ajar) or in an electric dehydrator (145°F). When the jerky is done, it will crack but not break when bent.

# Steak House Jerky

Prep Time: 10 minutes
Marinating Time: 8 to 12 hours
Drying Time for Oven: 4 to 6 hours
Drying Time for Electric Dehydrator: 5 hours
Yield: ¼ to ⅓ pounds of dry jerky

## Ingredients
- 1½ pounds venison
- 1 teaspoon seasoned salt
- ¼ teaspoon black pepper
- 1 teaspoon onion powder
- ½ cup soy sauce
- ¼ cup steak sauce

## Preparation
1. Rinse meat thoroughly in cold water to remove any remaining hair, blood, or other foreign matter. Trim all fat, tallow, and silver skin completely from the meat. Slice meat into ¼- to ½-inch thick strips with the grain.
2. Place all ingredients except the meat in a sturdy zip-top plastic bag. Close bag. Hold bag securely at the top, shake vigorously to mix ingredients well. Open bag, add meat, and shake vigorously until meat is well covered. Roll bag closed to remove as much excess air as possible. Allow to marinate in refrigerator for 8 to 12 hours, turning bag frequently.
3. Drain meat well in a strainer. Discard marinade. **DO NOT REUSE!** Blot the meat strips dry on paper towels.
4. Place meat on dehydrator trays or oven racks making sure not to allow the strips of meat to touch.
5. Allow the strips to dry in the oven (150 to 200°F with oven door slightly ajar) or in an electric dehydrator (145°F). When the jerky is done, it will crack but not break when bent.

# Aloha Jerky

Prep Time: 20 minutes
Marinating Time: 6 to 12 hours
Drying Time for Oven: 4 to 6 hours
Drying Time for Electric Dehydrator: 5 hours
Yield: ½ pound of dry jerky

## Ingredients

- 2 pounds venison meat, preferably the loin, round, or flank
- 2 teaspoons salt
- 2 teaspoons ground ginger
- 2 teaspoons brown sugar
- ½ teaspoon black pepper
- ¼ teaspoon cayenne pepper
- ¼ teaspoon garlic, crushed
- ½ cup pineapple juice
- ½ cup soy sauce

## Preparation

1. Rinse meat thoroughly in cold water to remove any remaining hair, blood, or other foreign matter. Trim all fat, tallow, and silver skin completely from meat. Slice meat into ¼- to ½-inch thick strips with the grain.
2. In a small glass bowl, combine all ingredients except meat. Mix well.
3. Layer sliced meat and marinade in a glass 9 x 12 casserole dish. Cover tightly. Or place mixed marinade ingredients in a plastic zip-top bag and add the meat. Massage the meat and marinade well to cover all sides of the meat. Roll the bag closed to remove as much air from the bag as possible. Refrigerate for 6 to 12 hours. Turn the bag or mix the meat mixture from time to time so the marinade gets to all the surfaces of the meat strips.
4. Drain well in a strainer. Discard marinade. **DO NOT REUSE!** Blot the meat strips dry on paper towels. Lay out on dehydrator trays or oven racks making sure not to allow the strips of meat to touch.
5. For a different experience, add a can of pineapple chunks to some reserved marinade. This should be done in a separate bowl or zip-top bag. The chunks can marinate the same amount of time as the meat.

6. Place the marinated pineapple chunks on trays with the meat in the dehydrator. The pineapple chunks will take longer to dry, perhaps a total of 10 hours. The chunks should be pliable when done.
7. Allow the strips to dry in the oven (150 to 200°F with oven door slightly ajar) or in an electric dehydrator (145°F). When the jerky is done, it will crack but not break when bent.

---

**JERKY FACTS**

- Four pounds of meat produces one pound of jerky
- Jerky is 75 percent protein
- Recommended as a light source of protein for hiking or trail blazing trips
- The more you chew, the more intense the flavor becomes
- Great after-school nutritious snack

---

# Smoke and Fire Jerky

Prep Time: 15 to 20 minutes
Marinating Time: 8 to 12 hours
Drying Time for Oven: 4 to 6 hours
Drying Time for Electric Dehydrator: 5 hours
Yield: ¼ to ½ pound of dry jerky

## Ingredients

- 2 pounds venison, preferably the loin, round, or flank
- ¼ cup red wine
- ¼ cup Worcestershire sauce
- ½ teaspoon liquid smoke
- 1 teaspoon seasoned salt
- ½ teaspoon garlic powder
- ¼ teaspoon black pepper
- ¼ teaspoon cayenne pepper
- Tabasco sauce to taste

## Preparation

1. Rinse meat thoroughly in cold water to remove any remaining hair, blood, or other foreign matter. Trim all fat, tallow, and silver skin completely from the meat. Slice meat into ¼- to ½-inch thick strips with the grain.
2. Place all ingredients except the meat in a sturdy zip-top plastic bag. Close the bag. Hold bag securely at the top, shake vigorously to mix ingredients well. Open bag, add meat, and shake vigorously until meat is well covered. Roll bag closed to remove as much excess air as possible. Allow to marinate in refrigerator for 8 to 12 hours, turning bag frequently.
3. Drain meat well in a strainer. Discard marinade. **DO NOT REUSE!** Blot the meat strips dry on paper towels.
4. Place meat on dehydrator trays or oven racks making sure not to allow the strips of meat to touch.
5. Allow the strips to dry in the oven (150 to 200°F with oven door slightly ajar) or in an electric dehydrator (145°F). When the jerky is done, it will crack but not break when bent.

# On The Range Jerky

Prep Time: 15 to 20 minutes
Marinating Time: 8 to 12 hours
Drying Time for Oven: 4 to 6 hours
Drying Time for Electric Dehydrator: 5 to 6 hours
Yield: 1 pound of dried jerky

## Ingredients

- 4 pounds lean venison from the loin, rump, or round, slightly frozen
- 3 teaspoons salt
- ½ cup brown sugar
- 1 teaspoon black pepper
- 1 cup red wine vinegar
- ½ teaspoon cayenne pepper
- 1 cup ketchup
- 1 teaspoon onion powder
- 1 teaspoon garlic powder
- 2 teaspoons dry mustard

## Preparation

1. Cut the slices about ¼ to ⅜ inch thick. Try to keep the slices as uniform as possible to ensure similar cooking times. Use a sharp knife or electric knife and cut thin strips against the grain of the meat for more tender yet brittle jerky. Or, if you prefer jerky that is more chewy, slice the meat with the grain.
2. In a large zip-top plastic bag or nonporous bowl, combine all other ingredients and mix well.
3. Place the meat strips in the bag with the marinade or in the bowl and mix well. Make sure all slices are covered with the liquid. Cover the bowl tightly or remove as much air from the plastic zip-top bag and seal closed. Let the meat soak in the marinade overnight in the refrigerator. Turn the meat a few times to ensure that all surfaces are covered by the marinade.
4. Preheat your dehydrator or oven at 145°F.
5. Remove the meat slices from the marinade and throw the marinade away. Pat the slices dry.

6. Dehydrator: Place the slices on the trays with room in between to allow air to circulate. Leave the meat in the dehydrator for about 4 to 6 hours, turning once after 2 hours.
7. Oven: Lay the meat strips on an oven rack. Prop the oven door open slightly to allow moisture to escape. Cook for about 4 to 6 hours. Turn the strips once after 2 hours.
8. After 4 hours, remove a few pieces and let them cool. Test them by bending the strips. If there is moisture present, let the meat cook a little longer. Remember that cooking times will vary depending upon the thickness of the meat strips and the air moisture conditions in your house. If the strips bend and do not break, they are done. If the strips bend and break, they have been overcooked.
9. Once the strips are dried thoroughly, let them cool. Then store them in an airtight container or vacuum seal them in plastic bags for longer storage.

# Spirited Caribbean Island Jerky

Prep Time: 15 to 20 minutes
Marinating Time: 8 to 12 hours
Drying Time for Oven: 4 to 6 hours
Drying Time for Electric Dehydrator: 5 to 6 hours
Yield: 1 to 2 pounds of dried jerky

### Ingredients

- 4 to 6 pounds of lean venison, slightly frozen
- 2 cups low sodium soy sauce
- 2 cups red wine, sweet
- 1 teaspoon powdered ginger
- 1 teaspoon liquid smoke
- 2 cloves fresh garlic cloves, minced
- 1 to 2 teaspoons McCormick Caribbean Jerky seasoning

### Preparation

1. Cut slices about ¼ to ⅜ inch thick. Try to keep the slices as uniform as possible to ensure similar cooking times. Use a sharp knife or electric knife and cut thin strips against the grain of the meat for more tender yet brittle jerky. Or, if you prefer jerky that is more chewy, slice the meat with the grain.
2. In a large zip-top plastic bag or nonporous bowl, combine all other ingredients and mix well.
3. Place the meat strips in the bag or bowl with the marinade and mix well. Make sure all slices are covered with the liquid. Cover the bowl tightly or remove as much air from the plastic zip-top bag and seal closed. Let the meat soak in the marinade overnight in the refrigerator. Turn the meat a few times to ensure that all surfaces are covered by the marinade.
4. Preheat your dehydrator or oven at 145°F.
5. Remove the meat slices from the marinade and throw the marinade away. Pat the slices dry.

6. Dehydrator: Place the slices on the trays with room in between to allow air to circulate. Leave the meat in the dehydrator for about 4 to 6 hours, turning once after 2 hours.

7. Oven: Lay the meat strips on an oven rack. Prop the oven door open slightly to allow moisture to escape. Cook for about 4 to 6 hours. Turn the strips once after 2 hours.

8. After 4 hours, remove a few pieces and let them cool. Test them by bending the strips. If there is moisture present, let the meat cook a little longer. Remember that cooking times will vary depending upon the thickness of the meat strips and the air moisture conditions in your house. If the strips bend and do not break, they are done. If the strips bend and break, they have been overcooked.

9. Once the strips are dried thoroughly, let them cool. Then store them in an airtight container or vacuum seal them in plastic bags for longer storage.

# Savory Ginger and Basil Jerky

Prep Time: 15 to 20 minutes
Marinating Time: 8 to 12 hours
Drying Time for Oven: 4 to 6 hours
Drying Time for Electric Dehydrator: 5 to 6 hours
Yield: 1 pound of dried jerky

### Ingredients
- 4 pounds venison, slightly frozen
- ½ cup soy sauce
- ¼ cup Worcestershire sauce
- ½ cup Italian dressing
- ¼ cup honey
- 1½ teaspoons minced garlic
- 1 tablespoon grated ginger
- 2 tablespoons chopped basil
- 2 tablespoons chopped thyme

### Preparation
1. Cut the slices about ¼ to ⅜ inch thick. Try to keep the slices as uniform as possible to ensure similar cooking times. Use a sharp knife or electric knife and cut thin strips against the grain of the meat for more tender yet brittle jerky. Or, if you prefer jerky that is more chewy, slice the meat with the grain.
2. In a large zip-top plastic bag or nonporous bowl, combine all other ingredients and mix well.
3. Place the meat strips in the bag or bowl with the marinade and mix well. Make sure all slices are covered with the liquid. Cover the bowl tightly or remove as much air from the plastic zip-top bag and seal closed. Let the meat soak in the marinade overnight in the refrigerator. Turn the meat a few times to ensure that all surfaces are covered by the marinade.
4. Preheat your dehydrator or your oven at 145°F.
5. Remove the meat slices from the marinade and throw the marinade away. Pat the slices dry.

6. Dehydrator: Place the slices on the trays with room in between to allow air to circulate. Leave the meat in the dehydrator for about 4 to 6 hours, turning once after 2 hours.

7. Oven: Lay the meat strips on an oven rack. Prop the oven door open slightly to allow moisture to escape. Cook for about 4 to 6 hours. Turn the strips once after 2 hours.

8. After 4 hours, remove a few pieces and let them cool. Test them by bending the strips. If there is moisture present, let the meat cook a little longer. Remember that cooking times will vary depending upon the thickness of the meat strips and the air moisture conditions in your house. If the strips bend and do not break, they are done. If the strips bend and break, they have been overcooked.

9. Once the strips are dried thoroughly, let them cool. Then store them in an airtight container or vacuum seal them in plastic bags for longer storage.

# BBQ Moose Jerky

Prep Time: 15 to 20 minutes
Marinating Time: 8 to 12 hours
Drying Time for Oven: 4 to 6 hours
Drying Time for Electric Dehydrator: 5 to 6 hours
Yield: About 1 pound of dried jerky

## Ingredients
- 3 pounds lean venison, such as moose sirloin, trimmed of all fat and connective tissue and slightly frozen
- 1 cup ketchup
- ½ cup cider vinegar
- ¼ cup brown sugar
- 2 tablespoons instant coffee dissolved in ½ cup hot water
- 2 tablespoons Worcestershire sauce
- 2 teaspoon dry mustard
- 1 teaspoon onion powder
- 1 teaspoon garlic powder
- ¼ teaspoon black pepper

## Preparation
1. Cut the slices about ⅜ to ¼ inch thick. Try to keep the slices as uniform as possible to ensure similar cooking times. Use a sharp knife or electric knife and cut thing strips against the grain of the meat for more tender yet brittle jerky. Or, if you prefer jerky that is more chewy, slice the meat with the grain.
2. In a large zip-top plastic bag or nonporous bowl, combine all other ingredients and mix well.
3. Place the meat strips in the bag or bowl with the marinade and mix well. Make sure all slices are covered with the liquid. Cover the bowl tightly or remove as much air from the plastic zip-top bag and seal closed. Let the meat soak in the marinade overnight in the refrigerator. Turn the meat a few times to ensure that all surfaces are covered by the marinade.
4. Preheat your dehydrator to 145°F or your oven to about 150 to 170°F.

5. Remove the meat slices from the marinade and throw the marinade away. Pat the slices dry.
6. Dehydrator: Place the slices on the trays with room in between to allow air to circulate. Leave the meat in the dehydrator for about 4 to 6 hours, turning once after 2 hours.
7. Oven: Lay the meat trips on an oven rack. Prop the oven door open slightly to allow moisture to escape. Cook for about 4 to 6 hours. Turn the strips once after 2 hours.
8. After 4 hours, remove a few pieces and let them cool. Test them by bending the strips. If there is moisture present, let the meat cook a little longer. If the strips bend and do not break, they are done. If the strips bend and break, they have been overcooked.
9. Once the strips are dried thoroughly, let them cool. Then store them in an airtight container or vacuum seal them in plastic bags for longer storage.

# Kate's Asian Grill Moose Jerky

In the mid-1990s, my husband, Peter, and I owned and operated a restaurant called PAPI's (Pete's-A-Pie International). We had a pizza operation in the front and a sit-down dining operation in the back of the restaurant. During this time, I was able to try different sauces and seasonings and tweak some recipes. Here is a recipe with an Asian sauce that has pleased the taste buds of many folks!

Prep Time: 15 minutes
Marinating Time: 48 hours
Drying Time for Oven: 4 to 6 hours
Drying Time for Electric Dehydrator: 5 hours
Yield: About 1 pound jerky strips

**Ingredients**
- 3 pounds lean venison, such as moose sirloin or top round, trimmed of all fat and connective tissue and slightly frozen
- 1½ to 2 cups of Kate's Asian Grill marinade (or one of your favorite commercially made Asian-type sauces)

**Preparation**
1. Cut the slices about ¼ inch thick. Try to keep the slices as uniform as possible to ensure similar cooking times. Use a sharp knife or electric knife and cut thin strips against the grain of the meat for more tender yet brittle jerky. Or, if you prefer jerky that is more chewy, slice the meat with the grain.
2. In a large zip-top plastic bag or nonporous bowl, combine the strips and the sauce and mix well. Make sure all slices are covered with the liquid. Cover the bowl tightly or remove as much air from the plastic zip-top bag and seal closed. Let the meat soak in the marinade for 48 hours in the refrigerator. Turn the meat a few times to ensure that all surfaces are covered by the marinade.

3. Preheat your dehydrator to 145° or your oven to 150 to 200°F.
4. Remove the meat slices from the marinade and throw the marinade away. Pat the slices dry.
5. Dehydrator: Place the slices on the trays with room in between to allow air to circulate. Leave the meat in the dehydrator for about 4 to 6 hours, turning once after 2 hours.
6. Oven: Lay the meat trips on an oven rack. Prop the oven door open slightly to allow moisture to escape. Cook for about 4 to 6 hours. Turn the strips once after 2 hours.
7. After 4 hours, remove a few pieces and let them cool. Test them by bending the strips. If there is moisture present, let the meat cook a little longer. If the strips bend and do not break, they are done. If the strips bend and break, they have been overcooked.
8. Once the strips are dried thoroughly, let them cool. Then store them in an airtight container or vacuum seal them in plastic bags for longer storage.

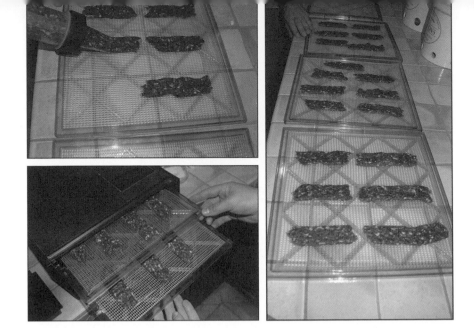

# Hi Mountain Ground Venison Jerky

I enjoyed the end product the first time I tried making jerky with a jerky gun. For those who are new to making jerky and want to try a simple method for making a consistent product, give this method a try.

Prep Time: 15 minutes
Marinating Time: 32 hours
Drying Time for Oven: 4 to 6 hours
Drying Time for Electric Dehydrator: 5 hours
Yield: ¼ pound jerky strips

## Ingredients
- 1 pound ground venison, no additional fat
- ¼ teaspoon nitrite
- 4 teaspoons Hi Mountain seasoning
- ¼ cup of water
- Additional Item: Jerky gun

## Preparation
1. Mix the nitrite and seasonings in the water. Place the ground venison in a mixing bowl. Pour the seasonings over the ground venison and mix well. Form the meat into a log. Refrigerate about 32 hours.
2. Place the meat into the jerky gun. With uniform pressure, make strips of jerky onto the dehydrator trays. Try to make them the same thickness and length. Give enough space in between the strips to allow air to circulate. Place in oven at 150 to 200°F with the oven door slightly ajar or dehydrator at 145°F. After about 3 hours, turn the strips.
3. After 4 hours, remove a few pieces and let them cool. Test them by bending the strips. If there is moisture present, let the meat cook a little longer. If the strips bend and do not break, they are done. If the strips bend and break, they have been overcooked.
4. Once the strips are dried thoroughly, let them cool. Then store them in an airtight container or vacuum seal them in plastic bags for longer storage.

# Ten Point Whisky Jerky

Prep Time: 15 minutes
Marinating Time: 24 to 48 hours (the longer it's marinaded, the stronger the flavor)
Drying Time for Oven: 4 to 6 hours
Drying Time for Electric Dehydrator: 5 hours
Yield: ¼ pound jerky strips

## Ingredients

- 1 pound of venison, such as moose, deer, elk, or caribou sirloin, slightly frozen
- ⅛ cup Worcestershire sauce
- ⅛ cup soy sauce
- 1 teaspoon hickory liquid smoke
- ¼ teaspoon garlic powder
- ¼ teaspoon onion powder
- ¼ teaspoon black pepper
- 1 tablespoon honey
- 3 to 4 tablespoons Ten Point Whisky

## Preparation

1. Cut the slices about ⅜ to ¼ inch thick. Try to keep the slices as uniform as possible to ensure similar cooking times. Use a sharp knife or electric knife and cut thin strips against the grain of the meat for more tender yet brittle jerky. Or, if you prefer jerky that is more chewy, slice the meat with the grain.
2. In a large zip-top plastic bag or nonporous bowl, combine all other ingredients and mix well.
3. Place the meat strips in the bag or bowl with the marinade and mix well. Make sure all slices are covered with the liquid. Cover the bowl tightly or remove as much air from the plastic zip-top bag and seal closed. Let the meat soak in the marinade anywhere from 24 to 48 hours in the refrigerator. Turn the meat a few times to ensure that all surfaces are covered by the marinade.
4. Preheat your dehydrator to 145°F or your oven to 150 to 170°F. Remove the meat slices from the marinade and throw the marinade away. Pat the slices dry.

5. Dehydrator: Place the slices on the trays with room in between to allow air to circulate. Leave the meat in the dehydrator for about 4 to 6 hours, turning once after 2 hours.

6. Oven: Lay the meat strips on an oven rack. Prop the oven door open slightly to allow moisture to escape. Cook for about 4 to 6 hours. Turn the strips once after 2 hours.

7. After 4 hours, remove a few pieces and let them cool. Test them by bending the strips. If there is moisture present, let the meat cook a little longer. If the strips bend and do not break, they are done. If the strips bend and break, they have been overcooked.

8. Once the strips are dried thoroughly, let them cool. Then store them in an airtight container or vacuum seal them in plastic bags for longer storage.

# POULTRY AND WILD FOWL JERKY
## Sweet Duck Jerky

Prep Time: 10 minutes
Marinating Time: 4 days
Drying Time for Oven: 4 to 6 hours
Drying Time for Electric Dehydrator: 5 hours
Yield: A handful of duck jerky strips

### Ingredients
- 4 ounces of duck breast, sliced with the grain about ¼ inch thick
- ½ cup brown sugar
- 1 teaspoon Adobo seasoning
- Salt and pepper to taste
- 1 teaspoon Runnin Wild warm spice

### Preparation
1. Mix the sugar, Adobo seasoning, salt, pepper, and warm spice together in a small bowl.
2. Place the duck breast strips on a plastic cutting board. Sprinkle half of the rub mixture over the strips. Press the seasoning into the strips. Turn the strips over. Sprinkle the remaining of the rub mixture on the strips. Press the seasoning into the strips.
3. Place the seasoned duck breast strips in a zip-top plastic bag and into the refrigerator. Turn once or twice a day to make sure that the seasoning is covering the strips.
4. Remove the strips from the plastic bag. Place the strips on the dehydrator trays making sure they do not overlap. Set your dehydrator or oven at 140 to 150°F. If using an oven, leave the door slightly ajar.
5. After 4 hours, remove a few pieces and let them cool. Test them by bending the strips. If there is moisture present, let the meat dehydrate a little longer. If the strips bend and do not break, they are done. If the strips bend and break, they have been overcooked.
6. Once the strips are dried thoroughly, let them cool. Then store them in an airtight container or vacuum seal them in plastic bags for longer storage.

# Black Pepper Ostrich Jerky

Ostrich meat is a healthy red meat with much of the flavor and texture of beef. Rich in protein and high in iron, ostrich meat is lower in fat, calories, and cholesterol than skinless chicken or turkey.

Ostrich meat is recommended by the American Heart Association, the American Cancer Association, the American Dietitians Association, and the American Diabetic Association, as well as many physicians.

Prep Time: 10 minutes
Marinating Time: 6 to 12 hours
Drying Time for Oven: 4 to 6 hours
Drying Time for Electric Dehydrator: 5 hours
Yield: ⅓ pound ostrich jerky strips

### Ingredients
- 1 pound ostrich fillet, all fat and connective tissue removed, slightly frozen
- 2 garlic cloves, minced
- 1 tablespoon onion, minced
- 2 tablespoons balsamic vinegar
- 1 tablespoon canola oil
- 1 tablespoon rice vinegar
- 1 tablespoon dark brown sugar
- ½ teaspoon kosher salt
- 1 tablespoon fresh coarse ground black pepper
- 1 teaspoon red pepper flakes

### Preparation
1. Slice ostrich fillet across the grain in strips ⅜ to ¼ inch thick.
2. Mix all ingredients except meat in a non metallic container. Mix well. Add meat to mixture. Allow to marinate in the refrigerator for 6 to 12 hours.
3. Drain meat well in a strainer. **DO NOT REUSE MARINADE!** Blot the strips dry on paper towels.
4. Place meat on dehydrator trays or oven racks making sure not to allow the strips of meat to touch.
5. Allow to dry in oven at 150 to 200°F with oven door slightly ajar or electric dehydrator at 145°F.

6. After 4 hours, remove a few pieces and let them cool. Test them by bending the strips. If there is moisture present, let the meat cook a little longer. If the strips bend and do not break, they are done. If the strips bend and break, they have been overcooked.
7. Once the strips are dried thoroughly, let them cool. Then store them in an airtight container or vacuum seal them in plastic bags for longer storage.

# Hotsy Totsy Pheasant Jerky

Prep Time: 5 minutes
Marinating Time: 3 to 6 hours
Drying Time for Oven: 4 to 6 hours
Drying Time for Electric Dehydrator: 5 hours
Yield: ¼ to ⅓ pound jerky strips

## Ingredients

- 2 pounds of pheasant breasts, slightly frozen
- ½ cup low sodium soy sauce
- ½ cup Worcestershire sauce
- 2 tablespoons hot sauce
- Reorder items so that these can fit in a single column
- 1 teaspoon garlic powder
- 1 teaspoon onion powder
- 1 tablespoon ground pepper
- 2 tablespoons honey

## Preparation

1. Slice pheasant breast across the grain in strips ⅜ to ¼ inch thick.
2. Mix all ingredients except pheasant in a non metallic container. Mix well. Add meat to mixture. Allow to marinate in the refrigerator for 3 to 6 hours.
3. Drain meat well in strainer. **DO NOT REUSE MARINADE!** Blot the strips dry on paper towels.
4. Place meat on dehydrator trays or oven racks making sure not to allow the strips of meat to touch.
5. Allow to dry in oven at 150 to 200°F with oven door slightly ajar or electric dehydrator at 145°F.
6. After 4 hours, remove a few pieces and let them cool. Test them by bending the strips. If there is moisture present, let the meat dehydrate a little longer. If the strips bend and do not break, they are done. If the strips bend and break, they have been overcooked.
7. Once the strips are dried thoroughly, let them cool. Then store them in an airtight container or vacuum seal them in plastic bags for longer storage.

# Kashmiri Pheasant Jerky

When there are successful days afield pheasant hunting, here's a tasty alternative to use up the extra birds.

Prep Time: 5 minutes
Marinating Time: 3 to 6 hours
Drying Time for Oven: 4 to 6 hours
Drying Time for Electric Dehydrator: 5 hours
Yield: ¼ to ⅓ pound pheasant jerky strips

## Ingredients

- 2 pounds raw pheasant breasts, slightly frozen
- 1 tablespoon McCormick's Garam Masala spice
- 2 teaspoons garlic powder
- 2 teaspoons ground ginger
- 2 teaspoons paprika
- 2 teaspoons turmeric, ground
- 1 teaspoon ground pepper

## Preparation

1. Slice pheasant breasts across the grain in strips ¼ to ⅜ inch thick.
2. Mix all ingredients except meat in a non metallic container. Mix well. Add pheasant to mixture. Press the rub into the strips. Wrap the strips in plastic wrap, place in refrigerator, and allow the flavors to set in for 8 to 12 hours.
3. Blot the strips dry on paper towels.
4. Place the pheasant strips on dehydrator trays or oven racks making sure not to allow the strips to touch each other.
5. Allow to dry in an oven at 150°F with the oven door slightly ajar or electric dehydrator at 145°F.
6. After 4 hours, remove a few pieces and let them cool. Test them by bending the strips. If there is moisture present, let the meat dehydrate a little longer. If the strips bend and do not break, they are done. If the strips bend and break, they have been overcooked.
7. Once the strips are dried thoroughly, let them cool. Then store them in an airtight container or vacuum seal them in plastic bags for longer storage.

# Lip-Smackin'
# Chicken Jerky

Prep Time: 10 to 15 minutes
Marinating Time: 8 to 12 hours
Drying Time for Oven: 4 to 6 hours
Drying Time for Electric Dehydrator: 5 hours
Yield: About 1 pound of chicken jerky strips

## Ingredients

- 3 pounds boneless chicken breasts, skin removed, fat trimmed off, slightly frozen
- 1 cup of your favorite barbecue sauce
- 2 tablespoons of liquid smoke to compliment the barbecue sauce
- 2 teaspoons Morton's Tender Quick salt
- 1 teaspoon hot sauce
- 1 tablespoon Worcestershire sauce
- 2 teaspoons chili powder

## Preparation

1. Slice the chicken breasts across the grain in strips ¼ to ⅜ inch thick.
2. Mix all ingredients except chicken in a non metallic container. Mix well. Add chicken strips to mixture. Cover the container tightly and allow to marinate in the refrigerator for 8 to 12 hours.
3. Drain chicken strips well in strainer. **DO NOT REUSE MARI-NADE!** Blot the strips dry on paper towels.
4. Place meat on dehydrator trays or oven racks making sure not to allow the strips of meat to touch.
5. Allow to dry in oven at 150°F with the oven door slightly ajar or electric dehydrator at 145°F.
6. After 4 hours, remove a few pieces and let them cool. Test them by bending the strips. If there is moisture present, let the meat dehydrate a little longer. If the strips bend and do not break, they are done. If the strips bend and break, they have been overcooked.
7. Once the strips are dried thoroughly, let them cool. Then store them in an airtight container or vacuum seal them in plastic bags for longer storage.

# Lemon Pepper Chicken Jerky

Prep Time: 10 minutes
Marinating Time: 4 to 6 hours
Drying Time for Oven: 4 to 6 hours
Drying Time for Electric Dehydrator: 5 hours
Yield: About ½ pound dried jerky strips

### Ingredients

- 2 pounds chicken breasts, boneless, skinless
- 1 tablespoon Morton's Tender Quick salt
- 1 teaspoon pickling salt
- 2 teaspoons garlic powder
- 1 tablespoon lemon pepper seasoning
- 1 teaspoon onion powder

### Preparation

1. Mix the salts and seasonings together in a small mixing bowl.
2. Slice the chicken breasts in ⅛- to ¼-inch thick strips. Line a cutting board with a layer of plastic wrap. Place the chicken strips down spaced about 1 inch apart. Place plastic wrap on top of the strips. With a mallet, pound the strips so they are all of uniform thickness. Remove the top plastic and sprinkle the strips with about half of the seasoning. Place the plastic wrap back on top of the strips. With a rolling pin or your hand, press the seasoning into the strips.
3. Remove the plastic wrap. Flip the strips over and sprinkle remaining seasoning on the other side. Put plastic wrap back on the top of the strips and press the seasoning into the chicken. Wrap up and set in refrigerator to allow the spices to meld for 4 to 6 hours.
4. Preheat the oven to 150°F or dehydrator to 145 to 155°F.
5. Place chicken strips on dehydrator trays or oven racks making sure not to allow the strips to touch.
6. Allow to dry in oven with door slightly ajar or electric dehydrator.

7. After 4 hours, remove a few pieces and let them cool. Test them by bending the strips. If there is moisture present, let the meat dehydrate a little longer. If the strips bend and do not break, they are done. If the strips bend and break, they have been overcooked.
8. Once the strips are dried thoroughly, let them cool. Then store them in an airtight container or vacuum seal them in plastic bags for longer storage.

# Umami Chicken Jerky

Prep Time: 10 minutes
Marinating Time: 4 to 12 hours
Drying Time for Oven: 4 to 6 hours
Drying Time for Electric Dehydrator: 5 hours
Yield: About ¼ pound dried jerky strips

## Ingredients

- 1 pound chicken breast, boneless, skinless, slightly frozen
- 2 tablespoons Worcestershire sauce
- 2 tablespoons low sodium soy sauce
- 2 tablespoons sake
- 1 tablespoon umami salt
- 1 tablespoon fresh ginger, minced
- 1 teaspoon onion powder
- 1 tablespoon light brown sugar
- 1 teaspoon dried red pepper flakes

## Preparation

1. Slice the chicken breasts across the grain in strips ⅛ to ¼ inch thick.
2. Mix all ingredients except chicken in a non metallic container. Mix well. Add chicken strips to mixture. Cover container tightly and allow to marinate in the refrigerator for 4 to 12 hours.
3. Drain chicken strips well in a strainer. **DO NOT REUSE MARINADE!** Blot the strips dry on paper towels.
4. Place meat on dehydrator trays or oven racks making sure not to allow the strips of meat to touch.
5. Allow to dry in oven at 150°F with the door slightly ajar or electric dehydrator at 145°F.
6. After 4 hours, remove a few pieces and let them cool. Test them by bending the strips. If there is moisture present, let the meat dehydrate a little longer. If the strips bend and do not break, they are done. If the strips bend and break, they have been overcooked.
7. Once the strips are dried thoroughly, let them cool. Then store them in an airtight container or vacuum seal them in plastic bags for longer storage.

# Buffalo Chicken Jerky

Prep Time: 20 minutes
Marinating Time: 4 to 6 hours
Drying Time for Oven: 4 to 6 hours
Drying Time for Electric Dehydrator: 5 hours
Yield: About ½ to 1 pound dried jerky strips

## Ingredients

- 2 to 3 pounds of chicken breast, boneless, skinless, slightly frozen
- 1 cup of hot sauce, such as Tabasco
- ¼ cup olive oil
- ¼ cup lime juice—fresh is best, but bottled is good, too
- 2 cloves of garlic, minced
- 2 tablespoons lime zest

## Preparation

1. Slice the chicken breasts across the grain in strips ⅛ to ¼ inch thick.
2. Mix all ingredients except chicken in a non metallic container. Mix well. Add chicken strips to mixture. Cover container tightly and allow to marinate in the refrigerator for 4 to 6 hours.
3. Drain chicken strips well in a strainer. **DO NOT REUSE MARINADE!** Blot the strips dry on paper towels.
4. Place meat on dehydrator trays or oven racks making sure not to allow the strips of meat to touch.
5. Allow to dry in oven at 150°F with the door slightly ajar or electric dehydrator at 145°F.
6. After 4 hours, remove a few pieces and let them cool. Test them by bending the strips. If there is moisture present, let the meat dehydrate a little longer. If the strips bend and do not break, they are done. If the strips bend and break, they have been overcooked.
7. Once the strips are dried thoroughly, let them cool. Then store them in an airtight container or vacuum seal them in plastic bags for longer storage.

# Turkey Gobble Up Jerky

Prep Time: 20 minutes
Marinating Time: 4 to 12 hours
Drying Time for Oven: 4 to 6 hours
Drying Time for Electric Dehydrator: 5 hours
Yield: About ½ pound dried jerky strips

### Ingredients
- 3 pounds raw turkey breast, slightly frozen
- ½ cup soy sauce
- 2 tablespoons lemon juice
- ½ teaspoon garlic
- ½ teaspoon black pepper
- 1 tablespoon grated fresh ginger

### Preparation
1. Slice turkey across the grain in strips ⅛ to ¼ inch thick.
2. Mix all ingredients except turkey in a non metallic container. Mix well. Add meat to mixture. Cover container tightly and allow to marinate in the refrigerator for 8 to 12 hours.
3. Drain meat well in a strainer. **DO NOT REUSE MARINADE!** Blot the strips dry on paper towels.
4. Place meat on dehydrator trays or oven racks making sure not to allow the strips of meat to touch.
5. Allow to dry in oven at 150°F with the oven door slightly ajar or electric dehydrator at 145 to 150°F.
6. After 4 hours, remove a few pieces and let them cool. Test them by bending the strips. If there is moisture present, let the meat dehydrate a little longer. If the strips bend and do not break, they are done. If the strips bend and break, they have been overcooked.
7. Once the strips are dried thoroughly, let them cool. Then store them in an airtight container or vacuum seal them in plastic bags for longer storage.

# Asian Turkey Jerky

Prep Time: 20 minutes
Marinating Time: 8 to 12 hours
Drying Time for Oven: 4 to 5 hours
Drying Time for Electric Dehydrator: 4 hours
Yield: About ¼ pound dried jerky strips

## Ingredients

- 1 pound skinned turkey breast, trimmed of all fat and connective tissue, slightly frozen
- ¼ teaspoon garlic powder
- 1 tablespoons fresh ginger, shaved in thin slices
- ½ cup water
- ¼ cup soy sauce
- 1 tablespoon Worcestershire sauce
- 2 tablespoons brown sugar
- 1 teaspoon ground pepper

## Preparation

1. Pound the turkey breast to make it as uniform in thickness as possible.
2. Cut the slices about ⅜ to ¼ inch thick. Try to keep the slices the same thickness and length as possible to ensure similar cooking times. Use a sharp knife or electric knife and cut thin strips against the grain of the meat for more tender yet brittle jerky. Or, if you prefer jerky that is more chewy, slice the meat with the grain.
3. In a large zip-top plastic bag or nonporous bowl, combine all other ingredients and mix well.
4. Place the turkey breast strips in the bag or bowl with the marinade and mix well. Make sure all slices are covered with the liquid. Cover the bowl tightly or remove as much air from the plastic zip-top bag and seal closed. Let the turkey breast strips soak in the marinade overnight in the refrigerator. Turn the turkey breast strips a few times to ensure that all surfaces are covered by the marinade.
5. Preheat your dehydrator to 145°F or your oven to 150°F.
6. Remove the turkey breast strips from the marinade and throw the marinade away. Pat the slices dry.

7. Dehydrator: Place the slices on the trays with room in between to allow air to circulate. Leave the turkey breast strips in the dehydrator for about 4 to 6 hours, turning once after 2 hours.

8. Oven: Place the turkey breast strips on an oven rack. Prop the oven door open slightly to allow moisture to escape. Cook for about 4 to 6 hours. Turn the strips once after 2 hours.

9. After 4 hours, remove a few pieces and let them cool. Test them by bending the strips. If there is moisture present, let the turkey breast strips cook a little longer. If the strips bend and do not break, they are done. If the strips bend and break, they have been overcooked.

10. Once the strips are dried thoroughly, let them cool. Then store them in an airtight container or vacuum seal them in plastic bags for longer storage.

---

**NATIONAL JERKY DAY**

June 12 is National Jerky Day. The first official National Jerky Day was in 2012. To celebrate this event, Jack Links, a major manufacturer of jerky products, created a jerky meat sculpture of the star of their advertising campaigns, Sasquatch.

In 2014, Jack Links commissioned artists to create Meat Rushmore out of three different types of jerky. After more than 1400 man-hours of labor and 1600 pounds of jerky, this meaty masterpiece was displayed in Columbus Circle in New York City.

---

Photo courtesy of Jack Links

# Fish Jerky
# Smoky Salmon Jerky

The preparation of this recipe includes the use of a smoker. Since salmon is a fatty fish, it is important to dry out the fish strips as much as possible. The combination of the heat of the smoker along with the smoke from the chips helps aid in this process. Remember that jerky will go bad quicker when there is still fat left in the meat or fish that has not been dried out.

Prep Time: 20 minutes
Marinating Time: 12 hours
Drying Time for Air Drying: 1½ hours
Drying Time for Smoker: 6 to 8 hours
Yield: About ¼ to ½ pound dried jerky strips

## Ingredients

- 2 pounds boneless skin-on salmon fillet, 1 inch thick or thicker, slightly frozen
- ⅔ cup sugar
- ¼ cup Morton Tender Quick
- 1 quart cold water
- 4 cups fine smoking wood chips

## Preparation

1. Cut salmon into strips along the length of the fillet, preferably ¼ inch thick. In a plastic or glass bowl, combine the sugar, Tender Quick, and water and stir until dissolved. Add the salmon strips to the brine. If needed, weigh the salmon down so it is completely submerged in the brine. Cover and refrigerate about 12 hours.
2. Remove strips from the brine and rinse strips well. Place strips on paper towels and dry as much as possible. Place them on smoking racks that have been coated with nonstick spray. Air dry the strips until there is a sheen on both sides. This can be done with a table

fan or in a cold oven with the convection fan turned on. This will take about 1½ hours.

3. After one hour, preheat smoker to 140°F. When the salmon is dry, place it on racks in the smoker. Place wood in the pan in the smoker. Close the smoker and maintain a temperature between 120 and 140°F until the salmon is firm. You may need to add wood to the smoking pan every hour or so. Total smoking time will be about 6 to 8 hours.

4. The jerky is done when there is no visible moisture on the surface. The strips will have a mild fishy odor, and the strips are not crunchy.

5. Once the strips are dried thoroughly, let them cool. Then store them in an airtight container or vacuum seal them in plastic bags for longer storage.

**DO NOT USE THE FOLLOWING WOODS FOR SMOKING:**

- Cedar
- Cypress
- Elm
- Eucalyptus
- Fir
- Pine
- Redwood
- Spruce
- Sycamore

Also, never use wood from a lumber yard or scraps of wood. Most times, you are unable to determine what kind of wood is being used for lumber. Second, more often than not the wood has been treated with some type of chemical preservative. Don't use wood from pallets, as the wood has usually been treated with preservatives. Also, most times you don't know what kind of product was loaded on it previously. Lastly, do not use wood that has any paint, stain, mold, or fungus on it. Not only will the food taste bad, but the smoke could also make you sick.

# Chipotle Lime Flounder Jerky

Prep Time: 20 minutes
Marinating Time: 1½ to 3 hours
Drying Time: 12 to 14 hours
Yield: ¼ pound flounder jerky strips

## Ingredients

- 1 pound flounder fillets, deboned, slightly frozen
- ¼ cup olive oil
- 2 tablespoons rice vinegar
- 2 tablespoons fresh lime juice
- 2 teaspoons lime zest
- 1½ teaspoons honey
- 2 cloves garlic, minced
- 1 teaspoon cumin
- 2 teaspoons Mrs. Dash Chipotle seasoning
- ½ teaspoon ground black pepper
- 1 teaspoon hot sauce

## Preparation

1. Place all ingredients except the flounder into a large zip-top bag, seal, and shake to combine. Cut the flounder into ¼-inch thin strips along the length of the fillet. Add the flounder strips to the bag with the marinade, reseal, and allow to soak for 1½ to 3 hours.
2. Drain the strips in a strainer. Place the strips on paper towels and dry as much as possible.
3. Lay the strips on the dehydrator trays so none are touching and dry for about 12 to 14 hours at 145°F.
4. The jerky is done when there is no visible moisture on the surface. Strips will have a mild fishy odor, and the strips are not crunchy.
5. Once the strips are dried thoroughly, let them cool. Then store them in an airtight container or vacuum seal them in plastic bags for longer storage.

# Aloha Red Snapper Jerky

Prep Time: 20 minutes
Marinating Time: 1½ to 3 hours
Drying Time: 12 to 14 hours
Yield: ½ pound snapper jerky strips

## Ingredients

- 2 pounds of fresh red snapper fillets, slightly frozen
- ¼ cup teriyaki sauce
- ½ cup soy sauce
- ¼ cup pineapple juice
- 2 tablespoons lemon juice
- 1 tablespoon light brown sugar
- ¼ teaspoon cayenne pepper
- 1 garlic clove, minced
- 1 tablespoon fresh ginger, grated

## Preparation

1. Place all ingredients except red snapper into a large zip-top bag, seal, and shake to combine. Cut the fish into ¼-inch thin strips along the length of the fillet. Add the snapper strips to the bag with the marinade, reseal, and allow to soak for 1½ to 3 hours.
2. Drain the strips in a strainer. Place the strips on paper towels and dry as much as possible.
3. Lay the strips on the dehydrator trays so none are touching and dry for about 12 to 14 hours at 145°F.
4. The jerky is done when there is no visible moisture on the surface. Strips will have a mild fishy odor, and the strips are not crunchy.
5. Once the strips are dried thoroughly, let them cool. Then store them in an airtight container or vacuum seal them in plastic bags for longer storage.

# Dill Cod Jerky

Prep Time: 10 minutes
Marinating Time: 1½ to 3 hours
Drying Time: 12 to 14 hours
Yield: ¼ pound cod jerky strips

## Ingredients
- 1 pound of cod fillets, skinned, deboned, slightly frozen
- 1 cup water
- 6 tablespoons salt
- 3 tablespoons sugar
- 1 bunch of fresh dill, chopped

## Preparation
1. Place the water, salt, sugar, and dill into a small saucepan over medium heat. Stir until the salt and sugar have dissolved. Remove from heat and let cool. Place the marinade in a large zip-top bag, seal, and shake to combine. Cut cod into ¼-inch thick strips along the length of the fillet. Add the cod strips to the bag with the marinade, reseal, and allow to soak for 1½ to 3 hours.
2. Drain the strips in a strainer. Place the strips on paper towels and dry as much as possible.
3. Lay the strips on the dehydrator trays so none are touching and dry for about 12 to 14 hours at 145°F.
4. The jerky is done when there is no visible moisture on the surface. Strips will have a mild fishy odor, and the strips are not crunchy.
5. Once the strips are dried thoroughly, let them cool. Then store them in an airtight container or vacuum seal them in plastic bags for longer storage.

# Old Bay Perch Jerky

Prep Time: 10 minutes
Marinating Time: 1½ to 3 hours
Drying Time: 12 to 14 hours
Yield: ¼ pound perch jerky strips

## Ingredients

- 1 pound of perch fillets with as many bones removed as possible, slightly frozen
- 1 cup water
- 3 tablespoons Old Bay seasoning
- 1 cup light brown sugar
- 1 tablespoon liquid smoke
- ½ tablespoon black pepper
- 1 tablespoon parsley, chopped

## Preparation

1. Place the water, Old Bay seasoning, light brown sugar, liquid smoke, black pepper, and parsley into a small saucepan over medium heat. Stir until the sugar has dissolved. Remove from heat and let cool. Place the marinade in a large zip-top bag, seal, and shake to combine. Cut fillets into ¼-inch thick strips along the length of the fillet. Add the perch strips to the bag with the marinade, reseal, and allow to soak for 1½ to 3 hours.
2. Drain the strips in a strainer. Place the strips on paper towels and dry as much as possible.
3. Lay the strips on the dehydrator trays so none are touching and dry for about 12 to 14 hours at 145°F.
4. The jerky is done when there is no visible moisture on the surface. Strips will have a mild fishy odor, and the strips are not crunchy.
5. Once the strips are dried thoroughly, let them cool. Then store them in an air tight container or vacuum seal them in plastic bags for longer storage.

# Savory Salmon Jerky

Prep: 15 min
Marinating Time: 1½ to 3 hours
Drying Time: 12 to 14 hours
Yield: About ½ pound salmon jerky strips

## Ingredients

- 2 pounds of salmon fillets, skin on, pin bones removed, slightly frozen
- ¾ cup soy sauce
- 1 tablespoon teriyaki sauce
- 2 tablespoons molasses
- 2 tablespoons freshly squeezed lemon juice
- 2 teaspoons freshly ground black pepper
- 1½ teaspoon liquid smoke

## Preparation

1. Place the soy sauce, teriyaki, molasses, lemon juice, black pepper, and liquid smoke into a large zip-top bag, seal, and shake to combine. Cut salmon into ¼-inch thick strips along the length of the fillet. Add the salmon strips to the bag with the marinade, reseal, and allow to soak for 1½ to 3 hours.
2. Drain the strips in a strainer. Place the strips on paper towels and dry as much as possible.
3. Lay the strips on the dehydrator trays so none are touching and dry for about 12 to 14 hours at 145°F.
4. The jerky is done when there is no visible moisture on the surface. Strips will have a mild fishy odor, and the strips are not crunchy.
5. Once the strips are dried thoroughly, let them cool. Then store them in an airtight container or vacuum seal them in plastic bags for longer storage.

# FRUIT AND VEGGIE JERKY
## Watermelon Jerky

**Ingredient**
- 1 seedless watermelon

**Preparation**
1. Cut watermelon and remove flesh from rind. Cut flesh into pieces about ¼ inch thick. If you don't have a seedless watermelon, remove as many seeds as you can without disturbing the flesh too much.
2. Place on lined dehydrator trays and dehydrate at 135°F for about 18 to 24 hours or until watermelon jerky is sufficiently dry and breaks when you bend it. If time allows, turn the pieces every 4 hours or so.
3. Store in airtight container or plastic zip-top bag.

# Honeydew Jerky

**Ingredient**
- 1 honeydew melon

**Preparation**
1. Cut melon and remove flesh from rind. Cut flesh into pieces about ¼ inch thick. Place on lined dehydrator trays and dehydrate at 135°F for about 18 to 24 hours or until melon jerky is sufficiently dry and breaks when you bend it. If time allows, turn the pieces every 4 hours or so. This may take a bit longer if the air outside the dehydrator is moist (i.e. if it's summertime and you live in the moist Southeast and the windows to your kitchen are open versus the same scenario in the dry Western states).
2. Store in airtight container or plastic zip-top bag.

# Kale Veggie Jerky

This is a variation of a tasty recipe by Jill Chen of Freestyle Farm (www. freestylefarm.ca). Jill is a multi talented artist and urban farmer living in Toronto, Canada. In addition to the varied animals on her farm, Jill grows and photographs her own food.

One large bunch or two small bunches of kale will yield about 1½ large zip-top bags of kale jerky.

## Ingredients

- 1 large bunch or two small bunches of kale
- 1 cup almonds
- ½ small onion
- 2 small radishes
- ¼ cup olive oil

- 3 tablespoons soy sauce
- 1 tablespoon mirin*
- 1 tablespoon lemon juice
- 1 tablespoon sesame oil
- 1 teaspoon sugar

## Preparation

1. Preheat oven to 250°F and line two cookie sheets with parchment paper. Or preheat a dehydrator to about 130°F for 10 minutes.
2. Wash, trim (remove the large stems), spin dry kale, and set aside. If needed, blot kale leaves dry with paper towels.
3. Pulse the almonds, onion, and radishes into a mealy texture in a food processor. Add remaining ingredients: olive oil, soy sauce, mirin, lemon juice, sesame oil, and sugar.
4. Blend well into a creamy soft texture adding water if necessary (one tablespoon at a time) to get a hummus-like consistency. The smoother the consistency, the easier it is to put a consistent layer on the kale leaves.
5. Massage the nut butter evenly onto the kale leaves. This will be easier if you wear food service gloves.

---

*Mirin is a sweet Japanese rice wine similar to sake but with a lower alcohol content and higher sugar content. If you don't have mirin, you can use sweet marsala wine.

6. Once the kale is well-coated, spread evenly onto the two lined baking sheets and bake for a few hours, turning occasionally so it dries out evenly. Watch the kale leaves to make sure they do not burn. If you use a dehydrator, turn the kale leaves every hour or so to ensure even drying.

# Maple Hickory
# Tofu Jerky

This is a delightful recipe for those who love jerky but would like to take a break from meat protein. This is also a tasty treat for vegans.

Prep Time: 10 to 15 minutes
Marinating Time: 1 to 2 hours
Drying Time: 6 to 8 hours
Yield: About ¼ pound of tofu jerky strips

## Ingredients
- 1 package of firm tofu (14 ounces), drained
- 4 tablespoons of soy sauce
- 1 tablespoon pure maple syrup
- ¼ teaspoon liquid smoke, hickory
- 1 teaspoon garlic powder
- 1 teaspoon onion powder
- Ground black pepper to taste
- ¼ cup hickory flavored barbecue sauce
- 2 teaspoons light brown sugar

## Preparation
1. Line a cutting board or bowl with two layers of paper towels and place tofu on towels.
2. Place two layers of paper towels on top of the tofu.
3. Gently press down on the towels to remove any initial water.
4. Replace the top damp towels with dry ones.
5. Carefully place a bowl, can, or other weight on top of towels to gently press down on tofu.
6. While the tofu is being pressed, in a medium bowl stir together the soy sauce, maple syrup, liquid smoke, garlic powder, onion powder, black pepper, barbeque sauce, and brown sugar until smooth.
7. Slice tofu into ¼-inch thick slices and place them in a plastic container that has a tight lid. Pour the sauce over the slices. Turn the slices so they are covered in the marinade well. Cover the container.

8. Place the container in the refrigerator and let marinate for 1 to 2 hours.
9. Oven: Preheat the oven to about 200°F. Line the oven rack with heavy duty aluminum foil and place in the lowest position of the oven. Place the tofu slices on the foil. Throw away the excess marinade. Bake for about 8 hours, checking and turning over tofu slices every few hours.
10. Dehydrator: Preheat the dehydrator for about 10 minutes at about 155°F. Line the dehydrator trays with parchment paper. Place the cut pieces of tofu on the paper-lined trays. Keep plenty of room between the slices for air to circulate. Plan for about 6 to 8 hours for the slices to dry. The overall time will vary depending upon the temperature setting, the humidity of the air in the room where you are drying, and the thickness of your slices.
11. Tofu jerky is done when it is hard and uniformly dark in color. Store the cooled tofu jerky in sealable glass, metal, or plastic containers.

# Far East Tofu Jerky

Prep Time: 10 to 15 minutes
Marinating Time: 1 to 2 hours
Drying Time: 6 to 8 hours
Yield: About ¼ pound tofu jerky strips

## Ingredients
- 1 pound firm tofu
- ½ cup low sodium soy sauce
- 1 tablespoon sake
- 1 tablespoon fresh ginger, grated
- 2 tablespoons fresh scallions, minced
- 2 tablespoons water
- 1 tablespoon honey
- ½ teaspoon red pepper, ground

## Preparation
1. Layer a cutting board or bowl with two layers of paper towels and place tofu on towels.
2. Then, place two layers of paper towels on top of the tofu.
3. Gently press down on the top of the towels to remove any initial water.
4. Remove damp top towels and place two layers of fresh towels on the top of the tofu.
5. Carefully place a bowl, can, or other weight on top of towels to gently press down on tofu.
6. While the tofu is being pressed, in a medium, stir together the remaining ingredients until smooth.
7. Slice tofu into ¼-inch thick slices and place them in a plastic container that has a tight lid. Pour the sauce over the slices. Turn the slices so they are covered in the marinade well. Cover the container.
8. Place the container in the refrigerator and let marinate for 1 to 2 hours.
9. Oven: Preheat the oven to about 200°F. Line the oven rack with heavy duty aluminum foil and place in the lowest position of the oven. Place the tofu slices on the foil. Throw away the excess

marinade. Bake for about 8 hours, checking and turning over tofu slices every few hours.

10. Dehydrator: Preheat the dehydrator for about 10 minutes at about 155°F. Line the dehydrator trays with parchment paper. Place the cut pieces of tofu on the paper-lined trays. Keep plenty of room between the slices for air to circulate. Plan for about 6 to 8 hours for the slices to dry. The overall time will vary depending upon the temperature setting, the humidity of the air in the room where you are drying, and the thickness of your slices.

11. Tofu jerky is done when it is hard and uniformly dark in color. Store the cooled tofu jerky in sealable glass, metal, or plastic containers.

---

**JERKY FOOD SAFETY**

Making your own jerky brings many rewards, including having control over what goes in to the product you are going to eat. Homemade jerky is an ideal treat for many sport enthusiasts as it is light, easy to carry, and can be made from many lean meats and fish.

Whenever preparing jerky, following these food safety guidelines:
- Wash hands thoroughly before handling raw food products.
- Keep raw meat and fish refrigerated until you will begin working with it.
- Always marinate food product in the refrigerator.
- Always wash cutting boards and utensils with hot soapy water after contact with raw food products.
- As an extra step in cleaning, sanitize all work surfaces and utensils with a bleach solution (1 tablespoon bleach per quart of water).
- Do not mix raw meat and dried jerky.

---

# Jerky Treats for Your Dogs

Jerky treats for dogs are fun to make. By making these treats at home, you are know exactly what your pet is ingesting. During October 2013, a consumer alert was issued regarding pet deaths from jerky products made in China. Numerous dogs became ill or died after eating jerky treats made in China. By the spring of 2014, many of the major pet chain stores were removing treats made in China to help stop this outbreak. As of this writing, the exact cause of the outbreak had not yet been determined. The FDA, however, is undertaking studies, many of which include necropsies to help narrow down the cause of these illnesses and deaths.

According to the terms of a settlement in a class-action lawsuit as of late May 2014, two of the United State's biggest makers of jerky treats that were blamed for deaths and illnesses of thousands of pets agreed to develop a $6.5 million fund to compensate dog owners who believe their animals were harmed by the jerky treats made in China. Nestle Purina PetCare Co. and Waggin' Train LLC reached an agreement with pet owners in several states who were seeking compensation for their claims of suffering and death of pets who ate chicken and other jerky treats made in China.

With that said, why not keep control over what you feed your pet? Here are a few simple pet jerky recipes that you can make yourself.

# Thai Chicken Jerky for Dogs

Prep Time: 15 minutes
Marinating Time: 4 to 6 hours
Drying Time: 6 to 8 hours
Yield: About ¼ pound chicken jerky strips for your dog

## Ingredients

- 2 or 3 chicken breasts, boneless, skinless, slightly frozen
- 1 cup organic coconut milk
- 2 teaspoons onion salt
- 3 whole fresh basil leaves
- 2 cups water (more if needed)

## Preparation

1. Chop basil leaves and combine with coconut milk, onion salt, and water in a large bowl.
2. Remove all fat and other tissue from the chicken breasts and cut into strips.
3. Place the chicken strips into the marinade, add more water if needed to cover the strips, and allow the strips to marinate for about 4 to 6 hours in the refrigerator.
4. After meat has marinated, pour meat into a strainer, allowing all of the marinade to drain from the meat. Discard marinade. **DO NOT REUSE!**
5. Place meat on dehydrator trays or oven racks, making sure not to allow the strips of meat to touch.
6. Allow to the chicken strips to dry in oven at 150°F or electric dehydrator at 145°F. When jerky is done, it will crack but not break when bent.

# Sweet Potato Jerky Chews for Dogs

Simple, plain, nutritious, and so easy to make!

Prep Time: 10 minutes
Drying Time: 6 to 12 hours
Yield: A handful of sweet potato jerky treats for your dog

**Ingredient**
- 2 sweet potatoes, washed and peeled

**Preparation**
1. Slice the sweet potatoes into ¼-inch slices length wise.
2. Preheat the dehydrator for about 10 minutes set at 145 to 155°F.
3. Place the strips on dehydrator trays evenly spaced apart. Place in dehydrator for about 6 to 12 hours. The time will vary depending upon the humidity conditions in the area where the dehydrator is set. Turn the slices every 2 hours or so and check for doneness after 6 hours. At about 6 to 10 hours, the slices should be dry and a bit chewy. If you want more brittle strips, dry another 2 hours.

# One-Two Chicken Jerky for Dogs

Many dogs love chicken. Here is a simple recipe to make chicken jerky treats for your favorite pets. You can be assured of the ingredients and the hint of garlic powder makes it tasty for your pooch. Please note that too much garlic is not good for dogs. Do not use more than is indicated without first checking with your dog's veterinarian.

Prep Time: 10 minutes
Drying Time: 4 to 6 hours
Yield: A handful of flavored chicken jerky treats

### Ingredients
- 2 skinless chicken breasts, slightly frozen
- ½ teaspoon garlic powder

### Preparation
1. With a knife or a food slicer, slice the chicken breasts in ¼-inch thick slices.
2. Place the slices in a plastic bag and sprinkle in the garlic powder. Mix the slices around to coat the chicken with the garlic powder.
3. Lay the strips on the dehydrator trays so that the slices do not overlap one another. Place the trays in the dehydrator set at 150°F.
4. Let dry 4 to 6 hours. Check after 3 hours for doneness. Turn the slices over after the initial check.
5. When the product bends and does not break, it is dry and ready as a treat.
6. Seal the chicken jerky treats in a plastic bag or plastic container with a lid.

# Marinades

Now that you have read some of the recipes for making jerky, this section was created so you can take the procedures from the previous section and change up the marinades. Remember that you don't need a lot of liquid marinade with meat, poultry, or fish. In fact, most times you can use a ratio of one pound of meat (or poultry or fish) to about ½ to 1 cup of marinade. Just make sure that the marinade covers all surfaces of the product.

Use your cooking knowledge to gauge which types of meat you will use each marinade with. As an aid, a key is included:

**B** – beef
**V** – venison
**F** – fish
**P** – poultry (including pheasant and duck)

Following are some guidelines for preparing and using marinades.

# Simple Rules for Marinating Meats

- Marinated meats and fish should always be refrigerated.
- Always marinate meats and fish in a non metallic container. The metal could react with the marinade and cause discoloration or even an undesirable taste.
- Fish takes on the flavor of a marinade much more quickly than meat. But fish can be in a brine for a day or two.
- When a marinade has been used with raw meat, the marinade should never be used again unless it is thoroughly cooked.

# Spicy Marinade

Prep Time: 5 minutes
Yield: Makes about 2 cups
Works with: BVFP

- 1 cup soy sauce
- ⅓ cup canola oil
- ⅓ cup brown sugar
- 3 tablespoons apple cider
- 1 tablespoon Tabasco
- 2 cloves garlic, minced
- 1 teaspoon minced fresh ginger

# Java Jolt Marinade

Prep Time: 10 minutes
Yield: 1½ cups
Works with: BVP

- 1 cup strong black coffee
- ¼ cup apple cider vinegar
- ¼ cup canola oil
- 1 jalapeño, seeded and minced
- 1 tablespoon ground smoked cumin
- 2 teaspoons dried oregano
- ½ tablespoon chili powder
- 1 onion, thinly sliced
- 4 garlic cloves, minced

# Asian Marinade

Prep Time: 10 to 15 minutes
Yield: About 2 cups
Works with: BVFP

- ¼ cup sake
- ¼ cup mirin*
- ½ cup low sodium soy sauce
- 2 tablespoons toasted sesame oil
- ¼ cup rice vinegar
- 3 garlic cloves, minced
- 2 tablespoons fresh ginger, minced
- 4 scallions, minced
- 2 tablespoons Sriracha
- 3 tablespoons brown sugar

---

*Mirin is a sweet Japanese rice wine similar to sake but with a lower alcohol content and higher sugar content. If you don't have mirin, you can use sweet marsala wine.

# Citrus Zing Marinade

Prep Time: 10 to 15 minutes
Yield: About 1 cup
Works with: VFP

- ½ cup apple cider vinegar
- Juice from 1 lime
- Juice from ½ a lemon
- Juice from 1 orange
- 2 cloves garlic, minced

- ½ small onion, minced
- 2 teaspoons roasted cumin
- 2 teaspoons chili powder
- 1 teaspoon salt

# Easiest Marinade Ever

Prep Time: 30 seconds
Yield: Varies
Works with: BVFP

- 1 to 16 ounces of your favorite Italian dressing

# Put the Lime in the Coconut Marinade

Prep Time: 10 minutes
Yield: About 1½ cups
Works with: BVFP

- 1 cup coconut milk
- Juice of 1 lime
- 2 tablespoons low sodium soy sauce

- 1 to 1½ tablespoons fish sauce (Thai Kitchen Fish Sauce is found in most grocery stores.)


# Apple Valley Marinade

Prep Time: 5 minutes
Yield: 3 cups
Works with: BVP

- 2 cups apple cider
- 1 cup extra virgin olive oil
- 2 tablespoons Cavenders All-Purpose Greek Seasoning

- 1 tablespoon minced garlic
- 1½ teaspoon freshly ground black pepper

# Smoky Marinade

Prep Time: 10 to 15 minutes
Yield: About 4 cups
Works with: BVFP

- ¾ cup liquid smoke, hickory or mesquite
- 1 cup Worcestershire sauce
- 1 cup soy sauce
- ½ cup lemon juice
- ½ cup orange juice
- ½ cup brown sugar
- ¼ cup canola oil
- 2 tablespoons freshly ground pepper
- ½ teaspoon cayenne pepper
- 2 garlic cloves, minced

Combine all ingredients. Stir well to dissolve the sugar. With about 4 cups of marinade, you will be able to marinate several pounds of meat or fish. Because this recipe includes liquid smoke, you do not need to put the meat or fish in a smoker, since the smoky flavor is in the marinade.

# Red Wine and Roses Marinade

Prep Time: 5 minutes
Yield: 3 cups
Works with: BVP

- 1 cup sweet red wine
- ½ cup virgin olive oil
- ½ cup finely chopped red bell peppers
- 3 teaspoons Mrs. Dash Italian Medley Seasoning Blend (or any Italian seasoning blend you have in your cupboard)

# Go Go Sriracha Marinade

Prep Time: 10 to 15 minutes
Yield: About 1 cup
Works with: BVP

- ¼ cup olive oil
- ¼ cup spicy brown mustard
- ¼ fresh lime juice
- ½ teaspoon chili powder
- 3 tablespoons low sodium soy sauce
- 2 tablespoons Sriracha

# Classic Venison Marinade

Prep Time: 20 minutes
Cook Time: 40 minutes
Yield: 4 to 5 cups
Works with: BV

- ½ pound raw carrots, chopped fine
- ½ pound yellow onions, minced
- ½ pound celery, including tops, chopped fine
- 2 tablespoons butter
- 4 cups vinegar
- 2 cups red wine
- ½ teaspoon parsley, chopped
- 1 bay leaf
- ½ teaspoon thyme
- 1 teaspoon freshly ground pepper
- ½ tablespoon allspice
- 1 teaspoon salt

In a medium sauté pan over medium heat, sauté carrots, onions, and celery in the butter. When the vegetables are soft (not browned) add the remaining ingredients. Bring to a boil, then simmer covered for ½ hour. Allow to cool.

# Dijon Mustard Marinade

Prep Time: 5 minutes
Yield: 1⅔ cups
Works with: BVFP

- 1 cup canola oil
- ⅓ cup Dijon-style mustard
- ⅓ cup rice wine vinegar
- 1 tablespoon fresh lemon juice
- Freshly ground pepper to taste

# Triple Pepper Marinade

Prep Time: 10 minutes
Yield: 1 cup
Works with: BVP

- ½ cup Worcestershire sauce
- ½ cup red wine
- 1 tablespoon salt
- 2 tablespoons tri color peppercorns
- 1 tablespoon red pepper flakes
- ½ tablespoon whole mustard seeds

In a small bowl, combine the Worcestershire sauce, red wine, and salt. Stir to dissolve the salt. With a mortar and pestle or in a grinder, crack or grind the peppercorns and whole mustard seeds. Add the mixture and the red pepper flakes to the liquid and stir to combine.

# Tried and True Marinade

Prep Time: 10 to 15 minutes
Yield: About 3 cups
Works with: BVFP

- 1½ cups vegetable oil
- ¾ cup soy sauce
- ⅓ cup apple cider vinegar
- ½ cup Worcestershire sauce
- ⅓ cup fresh lemon juice
- 2 tablespoons dry mustard
- 1 tablespoon freshly ground pepper
- 1¼ teaspoons salt
- 1 teaspoon dried parsley
- 1 teaspoon garlic powder

# Wild Turkey Maple Bourbon Marinade

Prep Time: 5 minutes
Yield: Just less than 2 cups
Works with: BVP

- 1 cup maple syrup
- ⅔ cup Wild Turkey bourbon (or whatever favorite bourbon you have)
- ¼ teaspoon ground cayenne pepper
- Freshly ground black pepper to taste

# Far East Marinade

Prep Time: 10 to 15 minutes
Yield: 1½ cups
Works with: BVFP

- ¾ cup soy sauce
- ¾ cup mirin*
- 3 cloves garlic, minced
- ⅓ cup sugar

- 1 tablespoon toasted sesame oil
- 1 tablespoon fresh ginger, minced

---

*Mirin is a sweet Japanese rice wine similar to sake but with a lower alcohol content and higher sugar content. If you don't have mirin, you can use sweet marsala wine.

# Sweet and Sour Marinade

Prep Time: 10 minutes
Yield: 1½ cups
Works with: BVFP

- ½ cup low sodium soy sauce
- ¾ cup canola oil
- 3 tablespoons rice vinegar
- 1½ teaspoon grated ginger

- 3 tablespoons honey
- 1½ teaspoons garlic powder
- 1 green onion, minced

# Zesty Molasses Marinade

Prep Time: 10 to 15 minutes
Yield: About 1¼ cups
Works with: BVP

- 1 cup molasses
- 1 tablespoon balsamic vinegar
- 1 tablespoon lemon juice
- 2 tablespoons freshly ground black pepper
- 3 garlic cloves, minced
- 1 tablespoon dry mustard
- 2 teaspoons fresh ginger, grated
- 1 teaspoon dried thyme
- ½ teaspoon dried red pepper flakes

# Orange Martini Marinade

Prep Time: 10 minutes
Yield: About 3 cups
Works with: BVFP

- 1½ cup olive oil
- 1 cup gin
- ½ cup orange marmalade
- ¼ cup dry vermouth
- 2 cloves garlic, minced
- 1 teaspoon dry basil
- 1 teaspoon tarragon
- 1 teaspoon black pepper
- 1 teaspoon salt

# Lemon Garlic Marinade

Prep Time: 5 to 10 minutes
Yield: 1 cup
Works with: FP

- ½ cup fresh lemon juice
- ½ cup olive oil
- 2 teaspoons dried oregano leaves
- 1 teaspoon prepared Dijon mustard
- 3 cloves garlic, minced
- ⅛ teaspoon ground black pepper

# Teriyaki Bison Jerky Marinade

Prep Time: 10 minutes
Cook Time: 5 minutes
Yield: About 1 cup
Works with: BVP

- ½ cup low sodium soy sauce
- ¼ cup light brown sugar
- 2 teaspoons fresh ginger, minced
- 1 teaspoon garlic, minced
- 1 tablespoon honey
- 1 teaspoon toasted sesame oil
- 1 tablespoon sesame seeds
- 3 tablespoons mirin*
- ¼ cup water mixed with 3 teaspoons cornstarch

Mix all ingredients in a small sauce pan over medium heat. Stir to dissolve the brown sugar. When product simmers, stir and remove from heat. Cool before using.

---

*Mirin is a sweet Japanese rice wine similar to sake but with a lower alcohol content and higher sugar content. If you don't have mirin, you can use sweet marsala wine.

# Gibson Marinade

Prep Time: 10 to 15 minutes
Yield: 3 cups
Works with: BVFP

- 1 cup canola oil
- 2 cups dry vermouth
- 1 large onion in thin slices
- 1 lemon in thin slices, seeds removed
- 1 whole bay leaf
- 2 tablespoons light brown sugar
- 1 tablespoon freshly crushed pepper
- 3 tablespoons fresh rosemary

# Lynn's Sweet Beer Marinade

Prep Time: 5 to 10 minutes
Yield: 2 cups
Works with: BVFP

- 12 ounces beer
- ½ cup Worcestershire sauce
- ½ cup light brown sugar
- ½ teaspoon salt
- ½ teaspoon black pepper
- ½ teaspoon garlic powder

# Kate's Spicy Beer Marinade

Prep Time: 5 minutes
Yield: About 1 quart
Works with: BVP

- 24 ounces beer
- 1 cup honey
- 2 tablespoons lemon juice
- 1 tablespoon light brown sugar
- 1 tablespoon dry mustard

- 2 teaspoons pepper
- 2 teaspoons chili powder
- 1 teaspoon ground sage
- 1 teaspoon salt
- 2 cloves garlic, minced

Note: Open the bottles of beer and take one sip from each bottle, just to "make sure they're fresh." Then blend all ingredients and your marinade is ready!

# Red Meat Marinade

Prep Time: 10 minutes
Yield: About 1½ cups
Works with: BV

- ¾ cup canola oil
- ½ cup beef stock
- 2 teaspoons balsamic vinegar
- ¼ cup soy sauce

- 2 tablespoons lemon juice
- 1½ teaspoons fresh ground black pepper

# Tropical Beef Marinade

Prep Time: 10 minutes
Yield: About 1 cups
Works with: BVFP

- ½ cup rice wine vinegar
- ½ cup pineapple juice
- ¼ cup light brown sugar
- 3 tablespoons low sodium soy sauce
- 2 cloves garlic, minced
- 2 scallions, minced
- 2 tablespoons red pepper flakes
- 1 tablespoon freshly ground pepper

# Piquant Citrus Marinade

Prep Time: 5 minutes
Yield: About 1cup
Works with: FP

- 1 tablespoon McCormick's Super Spice Grill Blend
- ½ cup orange-mango juice
- 2 tablespoons lemon juice
- 1 tablespoon lime juice
- 1 tablespoon cranberry juice
- 2 tablespoons canola oil
- 2 tablespoons honey

# Dry Cajun Rub

This rub works well with small cuts of wild fowl, such as duck and quail breasts. Slice the meat into jerky strips, then press the rub into the strips. Place in refrigerator 1 to 2 days. Turn bag occasionally to make sure the rub is on all sides of the meat. Then make into jerky as usual.

Prep Time: 5 minutes
Yield: 2 tablespoons
Works with: P

- 1 teaspoon Cajun Seasoning
- ½ teaspoon dried rosemary
- ½ teaspoon dried sage
- ½ teaspoon dried thyme
- 1 teaspoon garlic powder
- 1 teaspoon onion powder
- 1½ teaspoons seasoned salt

# Brett's Savory Venison Rub

At the Greater Philadelphia Outdoor Sports Show, my husband, Peter, and I met Brett Rossman. Brett was a fellow exhibitor for the week. He is an avid outdoorsman and ardent wild game cook. He offered to share his prized rub that he uses not only for making jerky but also for marinating game before slow roasting over the barbecue pit.

Prep Time: 10 minutes
Yield: 2¼ cups
Works with: BVP

- 4 tablespoons freshly ground black pepper
- ¾ cup garlic salt
- ¼ cup Treasure Island Smoky Chipotle Chili Powder
- ¾ cup smoked sea salt
- 1 cup brown sugar

# Stand by Fish Brine

Prep Time: 5 minutes
Yield: 2½ quarts
Works with: F

- 2 quarts water
- 1 pint low sodium soy sauce
- 1½ cups light brown sugar
- ½ cup sea salt
- 2 teaspoons garlic powder
- 1 tablespoon fresh ginger, minced

# Dry Brine for Salmon

Prep Time: 5 to 10 minutes
Yield: 2½ cups
Works with: F

- 2 cups packed brown sugar
- ⅓ cup pickling salt
- 1 tablespoon dry mustard
- 1 tablespoon celery salt
- 1 tablespoon black pepper
- 1 tablespoon paprika
- 1 teaspoon garlic salt
- 1 tablespoon cayenne pepper
- 1 tablespoon onion salt

# Waterfowl Brine

Prep Time: 5 to 10 minutes
Yield: 4 cups
Works with: P

- 4 cups water
- ½ cup sugar
- ½ cup kosher salt
- 1 tablespoon cayenne pepper
- 1 tablespoon dry mustard
- 1 tablespoon white pepper
- 1 tablespoon ground cloves
- 1 tablespoon ground allspice

# Pheasant Jerky Marinade

Prep Time: 10 minutes
Yield: ¾ cup
Works with: P

- ¼ cup extra virgin olive oil
- ½ cup white wine vinegar
- 1 tablespoon lemon juice
- 2 cloves garlic, minced
- ½ cup fresh parsley, minced
- 1 tablespoon fresh thyme, minced
- 1 teaspoon fresh rosemary, chopped fine
- Dash of red pepper flakes
- Salt and freshly ground pepper to taste

# Traditional Fish Brine

Prep Time: 5 minutes
Yield: 1 quart
Works with: F

- 4 cups water
- ½ cup kosher salt
- ½ cup sugar

- 2 large onions, sliced thin
- 2 tablespoons minced garlic

# Lemon Pepper Fish Brine

Prep Time: 5 to 10 minutes
Yield: 1 quart
Works with: F

- 4 cups water
- ½ cup kosher salt
- 2 tablespoons freshly ground pepper

- 2 lemons, sliced, seeds removed

# Piccadilly Brine

Prep Time: 5 to 10 minutes
Yield: 1 quart
Works with: F

- 4 cups water
- ½ cup kosher salt
- ½ tablespoon cayenne pepper
- 1 tablespoon whole mustard seeds
- ½ tablespoon whole allspice berries
- 1 teaspoon whole coriander seeds
- ½ teaspoon red pepper flakes or more to taste
- ½ teaspoon ground ginger
- 1 bay leaf, crumbled
- 1 cinnamon stick, broken in half
- 3 whole cloves

Place all ingredients in a pot, mix well, and bring to a simmer over medium heat. Remove from heat. Let cool. Use as brine for fish.

# Mediterranean Brine

Prep Time: 5 to 10 minutes
Yield: 1 quart
Works with: F

- 4 cups water
- ½ cup kosher salt
- ¼ cup fresh parsley, chopped
- 1 tablespoon oregano
- 1 tablespoon basil
- 1 bay leaf, crumbled
- 2 cloves garlic, chopped

# Tofu Marinade

Prep Time: 5 to 10 minutes
Yield: About 1 cup
Works with: F and Tofu

- ¼ cup plus 1 tablespoon rice vinegar
- ¼ cup plus 1 tablespoon low sodium soy sauce
- 1½ teaspoons Asian sesame oil
- 1 teaspoon granulated sugar
- ¾ teaspoon chili paste
- 2 tablespoons sake
- 1½ teaspoons fresh garlic, finely chopped
- 1½ tablespoons olive oil

# Citrus Peanut Marinade

Prep Time: 10 to 15 minutes
Yield: 1½ cups
Works with: BVFP

- 1 cup freshly squeezed orange juice
- 1 tablespoon orange zest
- 1 tablespoon lemon juice
- ¾ cup smooth natural peanut butter
- ¼ cup packed dark brown sugar
- ½ cup low sodium soy sauce
- 1 tablespoon peeled grated fresh ginger
- 4 medium cloves garlic, minced

# Double Buzz Marinade

Prep Time: 10 to 15 minutes
Yield: 2¼ cups
Works with: BVP

- 2 large garlic cloves, minced
- 1½ cups cola beverage
- ½ cup strong coffee
- ¼ cup mirin*
- 2 tablespoons ketchup

- 1½ teaspoons freshly ground pepper
- 1 teaspoon salt
- 1 teaspoon dried rosemary
- ¼ teaspoon Tabasco sauce

---

*Mirin is a sweet Japanese rice wine similar to sake but with a lower alcohol content and higher sugar content. If you don't have mirin, you can use sweet marsala wine.

Now that you have read recipes for making jerky and recipes for making your own marinades, try to make a marinade of your own. Here are a few suggestions of spices that go well together. Experiment! Add the spices to your taste and come up with a special recipe that your family will surely enjoy!

- Caribbean: lime juice, oregano, thyme, allspice
- Indian: crushed ginger, garlic, ground coriander, cumin, turmeric, red pepper
- Mediterranean: wine or vinegar, olive oil, garlic, oregano, rosemary
- Asian: soy sauce, garlic, ginger, sesame oil, mirin, five spice powder
- Southwestern: cider vinegar, onion, chili powder, cumin, oregano
- Scandinavian: oil, lemon, dill

# Sources

## GLOVES

**Med – Express**
(800) 447-0495
www.medexpressgloves.com

**Hand Care, Inc.**
(516) 747-5649
www.handcare.net

**Illinois Glove Company**
(800) 342-5458
www.illinoisglove.com

## DEHYDRATORS

**Bass Pro Shops**
(800) 227-7776
www.bassprocom

**Cabela's**
(800) 237-4444
www.cabelas.com

**Excalibur Products**
(800) 875-4254
www.excaliburdehydrator.com

**Nesco/American Harvest**
(800) 288-4545
www.nesco.com

**Ronco**
(800) 835-8668
www.asseenonamericantv.com

## VACUUM SEALERS

**FoodSaver**
www.foodsaver.com

## ALL YOUR JERKY-MAKING NEEDS

**The Sausage Maker**
(888) 490-8525
www.sausagemaker.com

**Eastman Outdoors**
(800) 241-4833
www.eastmanoutdoors.com

**LEM Products**
(877) 336-5895
www.lemproducts.com
Many of these items can also be found in Wal-Mart and Kmart stores across the country.

## WOOD CHUNKS AND CHIPS

**Alder Wood Chips & Chunks**
(877) 275-9591
www.bbqrsdelight.com

## KNIVES/CUTLERY/SHARPNERS

**EdgeCraft Corporation (Chef's Choice)**
(800) 342-3255
www.edgecraft.com

## PRE MADE JERKY SEASONINGS

**Hi Mountain Seasonings**
(800) 829-2285
www.himtnjerky.com

## VENISON AND OTHER WILD GAME

**Exotic Meats USA**
(800) 444-5687
www.exoticmeatsandmore.com

**Broadleaf Venison, USA, Inc.**
(800) 336-3844
www.broadleafgame.com

**Broken Arrow Ranch**
(800) 962-4263
www.brokenarrowranch.com

**DeBragga and Spitler**
(212) 924-1311
www.debragga.com

**Shaffer Venison Farms, Inc.**
(800) 446-3745
www.shafferfarms.com

# Jerky Glossary

**Aging** – Holding meat in a temperature-controlled environment to allow natural tenderizing to take place.

**Bacteria** – Tiny one-celled living organisms that are everywhere. They are found in the air, water, and soil and on bodies. Some bacteria can be helpful to us; other types can be harmful. For this book, we are concerned with keeping harmful bacteria at their minimum.

**Bottom Round** – This cut is found in the hindquarter of beef. It is usually a lean and tough piece of meat. Because it is lean, it is a good cut of beef to use for jerky.

**Brisket** – This cut of beef comes from the lower chest area. It is the cut of meat often used for pastrami or corned beef. It, too, can be used for making jerky.

**Brining** – Brining comes from the root word "brine," meaning salt. The water-to-salt ratio is 1:16 or 1 cup of kosher salt per gallon of non chlorinated water. Brines are typically used with white meat (poultry) and fish.

**Calorie** – This is a common unit of measure for food energy. The recommended daily intake of calories is between 2,000 and 2,500 calories. Many jerky products are low calorie (fewer than 80 calories per serving) but high in protein.

**Cattle** – Is another term for a cow, which can be male or female. A steer, on the other hand, is a neutered cow.

**Chopped and Formed** – An alternate method of preparing meat that is to be made into jerky. Instead of using a whole muscle, this process involves grinding meat and mixing it with a filler—some other type of meat—so it can then be formed into jerky strips and dehydrated. This method is much more common when using exotic meat, such as ostrich, emu, and alligator.

**Chuck** – A cut of beef that comes from the shoulder area. Chuck is one of the eight primal cuts. It is considered one of the more economical cuts of beef. It can, however, be a fatty cut. If so, it would not be an ideal cut of beef from which to make jerky.

**Curing** – Refers to the preservation and flavoring processes used to prepare meat, particularly beef and fish. Curing agents include a combination of salt, sugar, nitrates, and nitrites. Salt slows the growth of microorganisms and bacteria by drawing water out of the meat.

**Defrost** – The process of thawing frozen meat by increasing its temperature. Meat should be partially defrosted when slicing it for making jerky. When it is in this state, it is easier to slice. Never defrost frozen meat or game on the counter. Instead, use running water, the microwave at its proper setting for defrosting, or the refrigerator.

**Dehydrating** – The method used to preserve meat by removing as much water content as possible, which creates jerky.

**Dehydrator** – A small appliance used to reduce the water content of a food item. Dehydrators are used to help preserve foods such as fruits, vegetables, and meats.

**Elastin** – A type of connective tissue found in meats that doesn't dissolve when cooked.

**FSIS** – The Food Safety and Inspection Service (FSIS) is the public health agency of the US Department of Agriculture responsible for ensuring that the nation's commercial supply of meat, poultry, and egg products is safe to consume and accurately labeled. Any food containing more than 6 to 7 percent product goes through this agency's inspection process.

**Farm-raised** – Animals raised for sale or consumption under state regulations are usually farm-raised.

**Fillet** – A boneless tenderloin.

**Flank** – A cut of meat from the belly muscles of beef. It is generally long and flat and is a tough cut of meat. Because it is tougher, many flank recipes use tenderizing marinades or moist cooking methods to soften the meat. Flank is considered one of the more economical cuts of beef.

**Game** – This term refers to animals that are typically hunted, such as deer, moose, pheasant, and duck. While game meats are typically leaner than their farm-raised versions, they can be processed, butchered, and stored the same ways as store-bought meats. In addition, to keep bacterial growth at a minimum, field dress game animals as soon as possible to keep the carcass cool.

**Grass-fed** – Directly from the USDA: Grass and forage shall be the feed source consumed for the lifetime of the ruminant animal, with the exception of milk consumed prior to weaning. The diet shall be derived solely from forage consisting of grass (annual and perennial), forbs (e.g., legumes, *Brassica*), browse, or cereal grain crops in the vegetative (pre-grain) state. Animals cannot be fed grain or grain byproducts and must have continuous access to pasture during the growing season. Hay, haylage, baleage, silage, crop residue without grain, and other roughage sources may also be included as acceptable feed sources.

**Ground Beef** – Refers to beef that has been processed in a meat grinder. When you make jerky, remember to use lean ground beef. The fat in the meat can hinder the drying process and can also turn rancid more quickly than lean meat. Ground beef jerky can be made with a jerky gun or it can be made manually with a sheet pan, plastic wrap, and rolling pin.

**Jerky Gun** – A cooking utensil to make uniform strips of meat jerky. It looks similar to a caulking gun. A jerky gun has a tube with a plunger or press and interchangeable tips (i.e. flat tip for strips of jerky or a round tip for jerky sticks). Ground meat is placed in the tube and pushed through one of the interchangeable tips onto a tray prior to dehydrating.

**Loin** – The section of meat below the rib cage, toward the round or hindquarter of beef. Loin can also consist of the tenderloin, sirloin, and top sirloin. Although these are all considered separate cuts of meat, they all come from the same general section.

**Marbling** – The fat that is naturally found in muscle tissue. Venison has practically no marbling.

**Marinade** – To flavor by covering in seasonings and allowing time to rest. Most marinades are made up of three components: acid, oil, and herbs. The acid works by partially breaking down the meat proteins on the surface of the meat and creating openings where the flavor seeps in. Marinades tend to work better on fish and chicken since their muscle density is not as thick as in beef or other red meat. When a marinade contains an acid that is left too long with the meat, it can "cook" the surface, which will cause the meat to dry out. Depending upon the amount of marinade flavor you want in your meat, some meats can marinate for hours. The less dense cuts , such as chicken and fish, often take less time to marinate.

**Mince** – To chop into very fine pieces.

**Moisture** – Refers to the presence of water in a product. Moisture and oxygen are the main causes of mold formation on jerky products. Ninety to ninety-five percent of the moisture should be removed when preparing jerky. Jerky recipes should clearly state the cooking temperature and amount of time meat should be dehydrated to remove the optimal amount of moisture.

**Mold** – A fungi that can grow on jerky if not properly prepared or stored. If moisture is not adequately removed during dehydration or if the jerky is not stored in airtight containers, mold is likely to form on the jerky.

**Natural Beef** – The USDA defines natural beef as any meat raised for human consumption that has "no artificial ingredients; and is minimally processed."

**Nitrates and Nitrites** – These additives not only help kill bacteria, but they also give meat a pink or red color, as well as a unique flavor.

**Organic Beef** – According to the USDA, beef must meet specific criteria to be classified as organic Organic beef must come from a verifiable production facility that has information on breed history, veterinary care, and feed use. In addition, cattle must be born and raised on a certified organic pasture, fed only certified organic grasses and grains, never have received antibiotics or growth-stimulating hormones, and have had unrestricted access to the outdoors to be labeled organic. Lastly, it must be processed in a facility that is also certified organic by a third party.

**Processed** – Processed foods have been altered from their natural state, either for safety reasons or convenience. Processing methods include canning, freezing, refrigeration, dehydration, and aseptic processing. While the current trend is to eat minimally processed foods, not all processing is bad. When raw milk is processed into pasteurized milk, it is done for food safety reasons.

**Protein** – Groups of amino acids that are needed for the body to produce energy. You need protein for your muscles, bones, and the rest of your body. Exactly how much you need changes with age. Teenage boys need up to 52 grams a day. Teenage girls need 46 grams a day. Adult men need about 56 grams a day. Adult women need about 46 grams a day (71 grams if pregnant or breast-feeding). You should get at least 10 percent of your daily calories—but not more than 35 percent— from protein, according to the Institute of Medicine. Jerky is high in protein and provides approximately 13 to 18 grams of protein per 1 ounce serving size.

**Raw** – A food item at its most natural unprocessed state. Raw food is uncooked and not dehydrated at all.

**Rub** – A mixture of dry spices that is rubbed on raw food before it is prepared for added flavor.

**Silver Skin** – The shiny, silvery-white membrane that surrounds many roasts and large cuts of meat.

**Smoker** – A device used in food processing to expose cured meat and fish products to smoke for the purposes of preserving them and increasing their palatability by adding flavor and imparting color. The drying action of the smoke tends to preserve the meat, though many of the chemicals present in wood smoke (e.g., formaldehyde and certain alcohols) are natural preservatives, as well.

**Sodium Nitrite** – A food preservative added to some jerky products to counter-act discoloration of the product. Sodium nitrite also prevents the growth of bacteria.

**Tenderize** – The process of breaking down the collagen in meat to make it easier to consume. Methods used to tenderize meat include mechanical tenderizing, such as pounding it with a mallet, or chemical tenderizing by applying a meat tenderizer or soaking it in naturally occurring enzymes, such as those found in pineapple or papaya juice.

**Vacuum Sealing** – This is the process of removing all oxygen from a bag prior to sealing it. Vacuum sealing prevents molding and prolongs the shelf life of jerky.

# Recipe Index